BARRA

AND

THE BISHOP'S ISLES

Living on the Margin

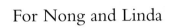

For Nong and Linda

BARRA

AND

THE BISHOP'S ISLES

Living on the Margin

Keith Branigan & Patrick Foster

TEMPUS

First published 2002

PUBLISHED IN THE UNITED KINGDOM BY:

Tempus Publishing Ltd
The Mill, Brimscombe Port
Stroud, Gloucestershire GL5 2QG
www.tempus-publishing.com

PUBLISHED IN THE UNITED STATES OF AMERICA BY:

Tempus Publishing Inc.
2 Cumberland Street
Charleston, SC 29401
1-888-313-2665
www.arcadiapublishing.com

Tempus books are available in France and Germany
from the following addresses:

Tempus Publishing Group
21 Avenue de la République
37300 Joué-lès-Tours
FRANCE

Tempus Publishing Group
Gustav-Adolf-Straße 3
99084 Erfurt
GERMANY

British Library Cataloguing in Publication Data.
A catalogue record for this book is available from the British Library.

ISBN 0 7524 1947 1

Typesetting and origination by Tempus Publishing.
PRINTED AND BOUND IN GREAT BRITAIN

Contents

List of illustrations

Colour plates

All colour photos are by the authors

Introduction

The tiny plane dropped through the thick cloud, buffeted by winds which had blown their way across the Atlantic. It had perhaps climbed no more than 2000ft since it left Glasgow, 50 minutes earlier, so by now it seemed it must be skimming the tops of the waves as it gently sank towards the invisible island ahead. But a glance out of the window revealed nothing but a uniform greyness that entirely surrounded the plane, below, alongside and above. One marvelled at the wonders of modern radar and navigation systems and hoped (prayed?) they were every bit as good as they were cracked up to be. The grey grew lighter, and there below us were the waves, not far below at all, perhaps a 100ft and getting closer by the minute. At 50ft they were still there. Then, a flash of white and with scarcely a bump we were down, not on the runway but on a great white shell-sand beach. This was Traigh Mhor — the world's only tidal airfield, on the Isle of Barra towards the southern end of the Outer Hebrides. An hour later the five of us were crouched behind a large boulder on the southernmost coast of the island, trying to shelter from a force eight wind that was charging in from the west, peppering us with horizontal sleet and hail. It was March 1989, and we were wondering just why we were there!

It was not at all like our colleague Richard Hodges had painted it. 'You'll love Barra' he said, 'it's beautiful and the weather's fantastic.' It was Richard's idea that our department in Sheffield should run a long-term project at the southern end of the Outer Hebrides. We were looking for an area where there was the potential for a long-term programme of integrated archaeological and environmental research in a marginal landscape. Our preference was for an area where there had been little archaeological research in recent times and the landscape was archaeologically unexplored. When Richard suggested the Outer Hebrides, the southern islands seemed to meet our requirements. But then Richard was appointed Director of the British School at Rome, and one of us had to take on organising the project rather than just being part of it, and KB drew the short straw.

Taking on the organisation of the project proved to be the easy bit. Far more difficult was coming up with a title for the whole project which on the one hand would convey what the project was about, and on the other would provide an easily remembered acronym. We thought long, hard and fruitlessly about this for six months; it eventually came to KB during a trip to Bangkok! And so the Sheffield Environmental and Archaeological Research Campaign in the Hebrides was born – SEARCH. Given the nature of our task, which required us to survey intensively ten islands and seek out their archaeological remains, this seemed a particularly appropriate acronym. It also gave us the idea for our logo – a stylised version of the Barrahead lighthouse, throwing light into the darkness. With this problem resolved we were ready to begin the SEARCH.

So, in March 1988 three of us took a reconnaisance trip. Based in North Uist, we looked at various locations in South Uist and then went on a day-trip to Barra, using the little ferry that runs between Ludag and Eoligarry. It was a marvellous day, with a blue sky, light breeze, clear air, and dolphins in the Sound of Barra. In a hired car we drove around Barra and were at once smitten with it. Richard was right – it was beautiful. But even superficially, at first glance, it was also quite different to the Uists. As the car passed Allasdale and swept round the corner towards Craigston, the Borve valley came into view and at that moment we knew that Barra was where we wanted to work and the Borve valley was where we wanted to start. Others of our colleagues preferred South Uist. But sure enough, three months later we were back with a team of students, beginning an archaeological survey of the Borve valley. This was to be the preliminary year for a five-year project which would end in 1993.

Thereafter, every summer for another twelve years our team worked on Barra and one or more of the islands to the south, which are part of the same parish. The episode in March 1989 was a brief one, lasting only a long, cold, wet week – but it was a very important one. While carrying out an emergency survey along the line of the long-awaited and suddenly imminent Vatersay causeway road, we discovered the complex of sites at Alt Chrisal, on the edge of the Sound of Vatersay. The excavations which began there in May 1989 continued every summer until 1999. Over the same period we systematically surveyed not only the whole of Barra and Vatersay, but also the four uninhabited islands to the south, and several of the small offshore islands too. We also excavated sites which were selected to try and enlighten our understanding of the monuments we were finding in the field.

This was a particularly necessary part of the programme, because the field monuments we were finding and recording were usually of unknown date, and in some cases of unknown type – that is, they were monuments of a kind we had never seen elsewhere. Field survey presented both opportunities and problems. Because most sites and monuments had been built of stone or at least involved considerable amounts of stone, they tended to remain visible in the landscape in a way that timber structures would not. Equally, by far the greater part of the islands' surface has never been cultivated, so that only a small number of archaeological monuments have been damaged or destroyed by agriculture.

On the other hand, many structures have been modified and reused, and others have been robbed of stone, particularly in periods of high population, for building field walls, barns, and houses. Again, the reason why so much land has never been cultivated is because it is covered in a blanket of peat, which must inevitably mask many early structures, particularly the less monumental ones. On and around the machair, it is not peat but sand which covers the old landscapes, and here we are dependent on the ever-changing configuration of the dunes to expose occasionally some long-lost site.

To these problems of discovery were added very considerable logistical problems when it came to working on the four uninhabited islands at the southern end of the island chain. With no regular ferry services to these islands, but only the tourist day-trips as and when the demand arose and the weather was suitable, supplying even a small team and its equipment on one of the islands was difficult and precarious. For the team itself, life was somewhat schizophrenic. Days in the sun surrounded by stunning scenery and colourful flora and fauna would be replaced with sudden unpredictability by fierce gales, horizontal rain, thunderous seas and all-enveloping clammy grey mists. At such times living under canvas lost its attractions and our minds inevitably turned to the question of just when, or how, the boat would arrive to take us back to the bright lights of Barra.

Even when we overcame both the logistical and the practical problems of discovering sites and monuments, we were faced with the further problem of dating them. Although some monuments – like passage graves and brochs – were of well-known types with a reasonably well-understood chronology, many others were not. Hut circles for example might belong anywhere between the fourth millennium BC and the second millennium AD. Other site types were new to us, like the hundreds of small rectangular and oval low mounds with stone settings on the high ground of Mingulay. What were they, and when were they constructed?

It was to help answer these questions that we undertook excavations on sites of all types over a period of twelve years. We excavated over 50 sites, although by no means all were fully explored; some sites were only sampled, in order to establish their identity but disturb them as little as possible. But here another problem arose: with a few notable exceptions, many of our sites produced little cultural material at all. The acidic soils ensured that animal and human bone did not survive except on those rare occasions when we were digging on sandy soils. Equally, the damp soils were not conducive to the good preservation of iron and bronze, and even pottery often rotted badly. So our excavations often yielded far less useful material than we had hoped, and even finding suitable material for C14 dating (and the money to have the material processed) was difficult.

Fortunately the scope of the problems we faced was actually somewhat reduced by the quantity of sites involved. When we began work on Barra, the total number of sites and monuments recorded on Barra and its islands was less than 80. Our final catalogue for these same islands now numbers almost 2000 sites. The large number of sites we have recorded has enabled us to develop a much better, more broadly-based, understanding of the similarities and differences between our site-types. Together with the evidence from 51 excavations, our observations and comparative analysis of field survey records have allowed us to ascribe many sites to a particular function and date with varying degrees of confidence. Some site-types remain problematic – smaller round huts and shielings in particular – and it may be that they always will. Nevertheless, we believe that we can now integrate the results of excavation and field survey to produce the outlines of an archaeo-logical biography of Barra and its neighbouring islands. That is what this book sets out to do.

In choosing a title and sub-title for it we have had to resolve two problems. Our choice for the sub-title was always *Living on the Margin*. We felt that this title reflected and emphasised both the geographical and economic marginality of the communities we were studying. In choosing the necessarily more explicit main-title we had to face up to a problem which we have side-stepped for the past 13 years: what do we collectively call the islands south of Barra? We have often referred to them amongst ourselves as the southern isles, but we have always been uncomfortably aware that the Norsemen used this term for the whole of the Outer Hebrides, as a counterpoint to the Northern Isles (Orkney and Shetland).

In this book, needing a term of convenience, we sometimes refer to them as the southern islands, hoping that the absence of capital letters and the subtle change from isles to islands will avoid confusion. We also speak of Barra 'and its islands' which is legitimate because all of the islands belong to the parish of Barra, and on other occasions we simply refer to 'our islands' which reflects no legal claim on our part but simply refers to those islands on which we have worked. But for the title of the book none of these solutions seemed appropriate and so we have fled to our last resort, and called them the Bishop's Isles. In the earliest description of Barra and its neighbouring islands, in the manuscript written by Sir Donald Munro after his visit of 1549, he refers to all the islands south of Barra as pertaining to the Bishop of The Isles, whilst Barra and the small islands to the north pertained to Macneil of Barra. As High Dean to the Isles at the time, he should know and we gratefully accept his word for it!

We faced the same uncertainty, though for different reasons, when choosing titles for the chapters. Whilst we have kept broadly to the traditional Neolithic, Bronze Age, Iron Age, Medieval, and Modern chronological sequence, we were aware that in the Outer Hebrides, even more than in other parts of the British Isles, the boundaries between these neat archaeological time-zones were blurred by anachronisms. We were also aware that the bronze of the Bronze Age in Barra and the Bishop's Isles is represented by one fragmentary cloak-fastener, and the iron of the Iron Age by a solitary spearhead and a few nails and lumps of slag. Metallurgy was certainly not a dominant feature of the islanders' life in later prehistory! The landscape on the other hand was, and always will be, a major part of life in the islands and it seemed to us that the changing human relationships with the landscape perhaps offered a more interesting series of chapter titles than those based on technological or historical terminology.

The writing of the book has been undertaken in much the same way as the research on which it is based, as a mixture of individual and joint effort. In undertaking the field survey of the islands KB took on Barra and Vatersay and some of the offshore islands close by, and PF led the teams on Sandray, Pabbay, Mingulay and Berneray. The same geographical division was observed in directing the excavations, with the important exception that PF also directed the many seasons of excavation at Alt Chrisal on Barra. Since geographical boundaries could not be easily accommodated within the proposed structure of the book, the division of labour has been chronological. Chapters 1, 2 and 5 were first drafted by PF and chapters 3, 4, 6 and 7 by KB. Completed drafts were then read by the other co-author who made comments, additions, and sometimes suggested alterations. The finished product is we hope relatively seamless and genuinely co-authored.

The book, however, is due to the labours not only of ourselves but also of many colleagues and students. On Barra and its islands for many years we worked alongside David Gilbertson and Colin Merrony. For shorter periods we were also assisted by Roman Krivanek and John Pouncett. The number of students who have collectively contributed to our knowledge of the islands is well in excess of 200, including a contingent of Czech students. Such numbers over so long were only possible thanks to the financial support of the British Academy, Hunter Archaeological Trust, Macneil of Barra Trust, Pilgrim Trust, Robert Kiln Trust, Scouloudi Foundation, Society of Antiquaries of London, Society of Antiquaries of Scotland, University of Sheffield, Western Isles, Skye and Lochalsh LEADER programme, and of course Historic Scotland. We are pleased to acknowledge the interest and support of Patrick Ashmore, Olwyn Owen and Noel Fujot in this respect. Logistics on the island were smoothed by our former student and now resident of Barra, Angie Foster, while we could never have visited, let alone worked on, the uninhabited islands without the generosity and seamanship of John Allan Macneil and Calum Macneil. To all of them we are very grateful. Our greatest debt, however, must be to all the people of Barra and Vatersay. From our first meeting with Macneil in Edinburgh in 1987, and our first season on the island in 1988, they have all welcomed us to their islands and allowed us to work unhindered on their land. It has been a great privilege and an unforgettable experience.

KB and PF
Isle of Barra
22 June 2001

1 Island landscapes

Before the age of television, 40 or 50 years ago, the wireless was probably the commonest form of passive entertainment in the home. However, one of the most regular and longest running broadcasts of that time was not in the field of entertainment; it was a service of specialised information aimed at just a small group of the British working population. They were the fishermen of our surrounding seas and the service was the fishing weather forecast. The majority of the listening public would not consciously tune in to it, but in time most would hear '. . . and now here is the fishing forecast at . . . hours GMT' and all that followed. Over the years, listening to the same ritual incantation of the forecast for the areas around the coast of the British Isles slowly impressed a string of, often exotic-sounding, names onto the sub-consciousness. Somewhere in between Rockall and Cromerty the name Hebrides would be imprinted. Unless you were familiar with the old black and white Bolting Brothers comedy film *Whisky Galore* from the novel by Compton Mackenzie this was perhaps the commonest means of becoming familiar with the name Hebrides and also to link it with a weather regime dominated by the pronouncement of such fearful prophetic predictions as 'gale force 9 imminent'. For a few others serving in Her Majesty's Forces the Outer Hebrides became more than familiar when posted there to man the military rocket range on Benbecula, also immortalised by Compton Mackenzie in his novel *Rockets Galore*.

There are several well-known early descriptions of the Hebrides, especially those of Sir Donald Munro (1549) and Martin Martin (1695), but it is Johnson and Boswell (1785) who may be described as the first recreational tourists to the region. The publication of their journey, although moderately well received, did not, unlike Queen Victoria's movements north of the border, instigate a popular trend of leisure travel in that direction. The intrepid literary pair did not actually reach the Outer Hebrides, but today the islands are a well-known and popular tourist destination. With the demise of the great herring fishing fleets, the difficulty involved in crofting for a living, and the lack of alternative employment, tourism is now probably the most important factor in the Hebridean economy. The islands and their oceanic environment are a total package of natural beauty replete with its own brand of flora and fauna presented in very available circumstances. Where else could one almost guarantee, in their natural settings, the sight (and the song) of seals, of puffins on parade, a display of 'Stuka' dive-fishing by gannets, the opportunity to photograph miniature orchids, cotton tails and carnivorous sundew plants, and the possibility of seeing porpoises and whales all on one day? Unfortunately this selection of wildlife should also include the notorious black fly or midge to dispel any thought of bias on our part.

The tourists naturally tend to be summer visitors either settled in the few hotels and the more numerous bed-and-breakfast houses or island hopping and camping out. Vatersay is the normal southern limit of this summer migration to the islands, although a few will take day-trips to Mingulay and Pabbay. A very few who are able to afford the sailors' life under canvas in private or hired yachts, like the Vikings, have the islands at their mercy, but they rarely stay more than a few hours, often not leaving their landing beach area and, if it is an overnight anchorage, rarely venturing from their cabins. Even Berneray at the southernmost end of the island chain comes within the compass of these fleeting, fidgety visitors.

The tourist months between May and August find the islands at their prettiest and it would not be too extreme to describe them at this time as precious stones. From the air they certainly appear like a scatter of emeralds bright green against a sapphire backcloth of shimmering iridescent blue of reflected sky. At some points at the edges of the islands the jewel setting of white gold can be glimpsed in the numerous beaches of shell sands. From this distance the islands appear very similar, but on closer inspection no two islands are alike; each has its own interests and it is impossible for an active mind ever to become bored with these island landscapes. The restless weather patterns that flow across the region ensure that every day can present a different view of colour, texture and, if the wind and rain should combine, solid reality. A windless day is a remarkable occasion and an extended period of still air is almost unthinkable; yet during the whole week of our survey on the island of Berneray in 1992 the weather can only be described as Caribbean. The soft blue of the sky met and merged with the crystal blue of the sea and each evening was a treasured glowing twilight of amethyst mist.

Such mythical weather introduces the other notable Hebridean subject, the black fly or midge. Our idyllic week on Berneray was glorious during the day, encouraging bare-skinned surveying, but the evenings were a hell of eating supper at a fast walking pace trying to stay ahead and clear of the pursuing black carnivorous swarm. The black fly may be thought to reside primarily in the many folds of the wild Iris flags which grow profusely in large patches which, if successful, can infest the landscape and smother most other plant life with their interlocked tuber roots. In fact it is only the contrast of the multitude of black specs against the bright yellow of the petals which gives this impression for in reality these little demons appear to inhabit every nook and crevice of the total environment. To the archaeologist, working crouched close to the ground intently concentrating on the soil as the archaeological deposits are carefully dissected at the point of a trowel, any significant lengthy drop in wind velocity spells disaster, for then the midges appear to surge up out of the very ground itself and within seconds the first maddening nips are felt. Whatever one's feelings towards these dervish of the insect world one has to be in awe of nature's ability to enable such minute creatures to survive so well in an environment that is notorious for its windy character (**1-2**).

Geologically the island chain may be considered as a single unit and this unity applies to most of the other natural attributes and characteristics. However one of the fascinating aspects of working among the islands is to discover the myriad

1 The priest's house Mingulay, from the east, in 1996

differences that give each island its own unique personality. In general the formation of the islands is the result of tectonic activity lasting several millions of years as the continental plate bearing Greenland began to move away from the European plate as the Atlantic Ocean was formed and expanded. An upwelling of magma resulted in the formation of the Outer Hebridean mountain chain composed almost entirely of Lewisian Gneiss, a metamorphosed grey-banded quartz-feldspar gneiss, sometime around 2900 million years ago. This mass was then penetrated by dykes and subjected to faulting on a considerable scale, but because it generally maintained a condition of isostatic equilibrium it attracted few further rock formations. Instead the original material was, over a period spanning millions of years, subjected to prolonged erosion forces that removed enormous amounts of material culminating in the glacial episodes that gave the landscape its final polish.

The result can be seen today in the naked polished and rounded rock surfaces exposed so frequently on the hillsides. So smooth is the surface and so frequent the lubricating rainfall that the thin mineral soils and spongy peat deposits find it difficult to remain in place and sudden landslips are not a rarity. The dyke system has also emerged as a characteristic of island landscapes even in areas where they have been masked by a mantle of soil and vegetation; they can still show as a linear dent in the ground. The basic rock in the dyke is more susceptible to erosion than the parent rock on either side resulting in a channel, sometimes tens of metres deep, with sheer

17

2   *The priest's house Mingulay, from the south, in 1997. The powerful winds that hit the islands have lifted the roof and blown down the front wall*

sides and a flat bottom arrowing across the landscape. These natural straight grooves have been extensively utilised by man, sometimes forming both convenient boundary lines and easy routes of passage through the hills. They are frequently incorporated into more recent enclosures, substituting for the drystone walling that is normally used where no natural formation is convenient, parcelling the landscape up into infield and outfield blocks, although they are rarely used for the main head dyke boundary of such systems. At the sea margins wave action cuts them back inland forming sheltered landing places around the rocky shores, but where the sea cliffs are high and the dyke narrow it can be eroded out while still maintaining a thin roof of soil forming a sort of sea cave. As such they can be a trap for the unwary who walk out onto the unsupported edge.

So we have an igneous bedrock, subjected to prolonged erosion in the past, swept clean and polished in the ice ages with only a few deposits of a glacially derived soil in exchange, a weather regime that dictates rain for most occasions, a latitude that limits the growing season. With such a set of pre-conditions it is little surprise that the soil, where it has actually managed to accumulate, is acid, mineralised and poor. Dominated by the formation of blanket peat that in extremes becomes a floating bog, and with much of the land surface steeply angled, it is a landscape little suited to arable farming, and sheep and cattle raising must have been the dominant form of land-based subsistence from a very early time.

This rather forbidding description can be applied to all of the islands but fortunately some are blessed with a remarkable landscape form called the machair, which is derived from wind-blown shell sand that can transform the acid, black peat soil into something quite different – a fertile brown calcareous soil, well suited for stock grazing and arable use. Machair is found extensively on Barra and Vatersay, and to a lesser degree on all of the other main islands. Since the underlying basic bedrock is all of Lewisian gneiss, with no other substantial rock type to provide the appropriate mixed sandy material, the beaches, where they exist, should be formed of cobbles and pebbles of gneiss. Such deposits do in fact occur, usually in sea dykes where the wave action is aggressive, and in the bays high above the normal tidal reach of the sea in the form of storm deposits. However this is essentially a drowned land/seascape with shallow waters covering what was at one time at low coastal plain. Such waters are the natural habitat for cockle shellfish, which have populated these waters in their millions. Since the submergence of these low landscapes at the end of the Ice Age the cockle shells accumulated, generation upon generation, being ground and pounded into tiny fragments and then compacted to form extensive thick beds. It is this fragmented shell that forms the material which give the bays their shining white beaches. The legendary Hebridean wind then takes a hand. Blowing in from the sea it sifts and shifts the grains of shell up the beach to form dune systems, some of which have become stable and extensive enough to harbour their own peculiar environment.

Stability in such a gale-ridden region is a constant war between the wind and the tenacious marram grass whose roots try to hold the surface of the dunes together. In the cause of this conflict the islanders have added barricades of sand-filled oil drums and the miscellaneous wreckage of our civilisation – gutted vehicles, worn-out electrical appliances and other metallic/plastic scrap, a tangled motorway pile-up of debris forlornly sinking beneath the sands. On dry stormy days the defences are overwhelmed and instead of a hissing whisper of sand passing between the stiff marram grass stalks the sand is lifted into the air and plastered over the hinterland beyond the beach and its sibling dunes. This then becomes the machair, the quality land of the islands, rich in wild flowers and butterflies and the preferred residence of the vast island rabbit population. The only one of our islands not blessed with machair is Berneray at the very southern tip of the island chain.

The mention of Berneray, or Barra Head, introduces a convenient place to begin a description of the individual southern islands, visiting each in turn in a northerly procession (**3**). The Hebridean island chain stretches for 208km from north to south with each island generally becoming larger and wider towards the north. At the southern end, Berneray is an appropriately wedge-shaped block of rock like a massive door stop supporting the islands above. Of the formerly inhabited southern islands Berneray is the smallest, only 3km long east to west and 1.3km north to south, and geographically the remotest which may give rise to the natural misconception often held by mainlanders that it is consequently the least likely to be able to support a stable resident population.

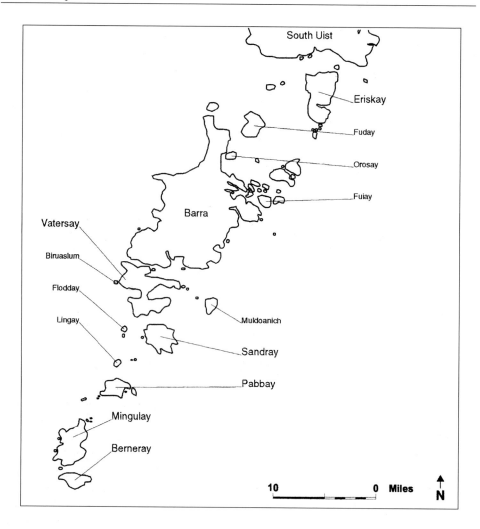

3 Map of Barra and the Bishop's Isles; all the islands from Fuday to Berneray have been surveyed by the authors except for Flodday and Lingay

Unless approaching by private yacht the first view of the island is usually from the north (**colour plate 1**) as one travels down from Barra passing all the other islands in our group, Vatersay, Sandray, Pabbay and Mingulay, in turn. The immediate impression is how green it looks. This is due to the northern aspect being the angled face of the wedge, the southern coast being sheer cliff along its whole length. One is therefore viewing more of the surface of the island than is usual. The angled surface allows better drainage encouraging a verdant growth of grass accounting for over 60 per cent of the land surface and providing some excellent rough grazing pasture while at the same time restricting peat formation to an absolute minimum, to such an extent that the islanders had to bring peat for their fuel requirements from the more abundant deposits of Mingulay.

The shore line is entirely rocky with 70 per cent being composed of sheer cliff faces, which next to St Kilda and Mingulay are probably the most spectacular in the Western Isle and are home to thousands of sea birds. Only 20 per cent, mostly along the northern side of the island, is of low shelving rock where even here there are few sheltered landing places. The presence of the Barra Head lighthouse on the 190m high cliff top at the western end of the island did ensure that a concrete jetty was constructed in a small inlet that even possesses the island's only minute cobble storm beach. But even here, unless the weather is right and the timing with the tide good, landing can be a hazardous business as the concrete is turned into a skating rink by exposed seaweed and algae.

With the axis of the island being west to east the long wedge-shaped profile offers little protection to the westerly gales, and any normal human settlement must always have concentrated around a slight depression and in-turn of the contour line on the north-eastern aspect. Not distinct enough to be called a valley, but just enough shelter to become a 'preferred place', it is here that one finds the focus of the community from at least early Christian times – the chapel, cemetery and most of the houses. This is in stark contrast with the apparent focus of life in the Iron Age, the massive galleried Dun that keeps the lighthouse company up on that most exposed westerly position with a further possible Iron Age defended retreat, Dun Briste, perched on another western cliff top promontory at a slightly lower altitude (**colour plate 2**).

To choose such locations in the Iron Age is almost a direct challenge to nature, for although the Hebridean weather is notorious, the meteorological ferocity that has been experienced on Berneray in historical times, especially by the lighthouse keepers and their families before automation displaced them, has entered the realms of legend. The author Miss Isabella Bird, best known for her travelogue recounting her journey through the Rocky Mountains of America, visited Berneray in 1863. No doubt following Dr Johnson's example as a literary person on tour, she has left us an account of that visit, during which she was told by the lighthouse keepers about the times when it was impossible to venture outside 'without the risk of being blown over the cliffs – the fate of a former keeper'. There is also the tale of the occasions when the lighthouse enclosure must be drained because 'it is so full of water from the drifting surf that they open the scuppers to let it out'. Robert Stevenson, the designer of the lighthouse, reported of an occasion when one of the hauliers on a horse and cart bringing materials to the construction site was blown into the air and both shafts of the cart broken.

Whether or not Berneray was continuously occupied is debatable. The presence of monuments that appear to represent most of the pre-Christian periods suggests that such a possibility exists, although in modern times the island has been deserted. Berneray may be the only island of our group that was never able to maintain any sort of tree cover because of its exposed situation, and with an absence of workable peat deposits fuel would always have been a problem, but in other respects the resources are certainly available to sustain a small community in permanent residence. The surrounding sea was especially noted for its rich fishing potential; William Chambers noted in 1866 that it was 'not a half or one tenth part fished', with ling and cod 'jostling each other in their anxiety to be caught and eaten'. Chambers does not appear to be aware that at this time up to 20 fishermen from neighbouring islands were often in temporary occupation while fishing the area. The seabird population and its eggs was also a rich protein source with puffins, guillemots, razorbills, fulmars and kittiwakes being commonly caught. Their feathers were also sold for bedding. In the nineteenth century sheep, goats, cattle and ponies were kept. There is little reason to suspect that in earlier times the resources would have been any different or less.

Further north on the island of Mingulay, and indeed all of the other larger islands, the possibility of continuous settlement is visibly more evident both in natural features and in the monuments found there. Mingulay is the largest of the uninhabited islands, basically oval in shape, but pinched in at the waist by the broad Mingulay bay on the east side (**colour plate 4**) and the narrow cleft of Bágh na h-Aoineig on the west. At various points peninsulas, inlets, headlands and clefts, along with a number of small outlying islets, provide a varied and interestingly irregular coastline. The core of the island is the broad amphitheatre valley that backs the eastern bay with its long sandy crescent beach. Surrounding the valley is a semi-circle of massive, steeply-sloped, round-topped hills: Hecla 219m, Carnan 273m, Tom á Mhaide 173m and Macphee's Hill. Easy access to the sea, shelter by the hills from the westerly gales, a broad relatively flat valley bottom with a fertile soil impregnated with calcareous shell sand from the beach, and a backing of dunes, are conditions that inevitably make this the prime preferred settlement location. This is borne out by the presence of a deserted early modern settlement just above the littoral zone (**colour plate 5**). The village includes a cemetery of almost certain early Christian date, an Iron Age stone building with deeply stratified deposits, and several cairns and standing stones of even earlier date. The upper beach appears to be actively trying to establish a dune system within the village area, and has been slowly engulfing the roofless houses there, while at the same time, according to the local shepherds, the dunes to the north of the village which have grown up in the past 40 years are now rapidly deflating revealing old, possibly prehistoric, land surfaces from which a number of Neolithic or Bronze Age worked flints were recovered. The good soil of the valley bottom appears clear of structural elements apart from field division walls and stone clearance piles, but at the back of the valley against the base of Tom á Mhaide hill is a large kerbed cairn, and deep in a soil test-pit cut into the valley floor was found a broken perforated stone mace head, presumably of Bronze Age date.

The sand blown from the beach and dunes also reached the lower southern slopes of Macphee's Hill producing a soil regime suitable for machair type vegetation growth. Erosion spots and sand ejected from rabbit burrows in this area produced a significant number of possible medieval pottery sherds which are most likely to be derived from additional manure applications. This suggests that at least in some periods agricultural advantage was also taken of this natural enhancement of the landscape even on the steeper slopes. This is borne out to a certain extent by a description of Mingulay dating from the sixteenth century which notes that the island was 'well manured, good for fishing and corn'.

Two other valleys form the remainder of the major lowland topographical elements of the island. A west-facing bay stretching between Tom á Mhaide and Macphee's Hill has a generally steeply sloped valley down to a sea cliff, but its exposed westerly aspect makes it an unlikely area for settlement which is underlined by the almost total absence of monuments of any description. However its slopes are well drained and provide a good rough pasture land with a rich growth of grass. The other valley, Skipisdale, faces the island of Berneray to the south, and is well sheltered by a low hill on the western side. The shore line is rocky with only a few inlet dyke formations maintaining storm beach cobble, but no shell sand. The lack of beach and dune systems results in no soil enrichment to the broad valley beyond. However, vegetation on the valley floor shows some signs of enrichment and improvement and a manuring strategy may have been undertaken in the past. Human activity is considerable, but not as intense as in the east bay area. There are two multi-period settlement complexes in the central valley floor area and a further one constructed on the lower valley hill slope to the north. A possible Neolithic chambered tomb stands dismally wrecked and robbed of its stonework on a knoll close to the shore.

Mingulay is notable for the number of smaller islands and stacks close around its coastline, but only Dun Mhor, between Mingulay and Berneray, was ever put to long-term use. Although its sides appear sheer the top is accessible and some square-shaped stone buildings can be seen there; unfortunately their function and age are not known since we were unable to include them in our survey work.

Of the coastal features the fat peninsula of Dun Mingulay jutting out to the west is cartographically the most prominent (**colour plate 3**). Surrounded on all sides by steep cliffs and enclosed across its dyke-formed neck with a low undated stone wall, it has been called a fort of Iron Age date, but whether it is actually either defensive or of Iron Age date is purely conjectural. For sheer magnitude of scale, plus an atmospheric sense of eerie heart-stopping menace, combined with plain breathtaking beauty, the monumental cliff face of the cleft at Bágh na h-Aoineig cannot be rivalled, even by the higher cliffs of St Kilda. There are several possible approaches, but perhaps the most arresting is to walk along the high valley ridge from Macphee's Hill to Tom á Mhaide. As one approaches, the cliff face rears up to fill one's whole perception – it dominates and beats you down. Finally on reaching the edge you can fearfully peer down to the small waves beating soundlessly far below. Suddenly the world is full of smell instead of sight – it is as though the door of a mausoleum has opened and a coldness numbs the brain and a thick stench gags the throat. The drop in temperature is of course the sea breeze welling up the chimney of the cleft, and the stench is the smell of guano as a million birds defecate on the ledges of the cliff face. At this time you may suddenly become aware of those birds, like patrons of the opera packing the balconies and boxes, all smartly and similarly dressed in black and white evening attire. Every now and again one will suddenly soar vertically upwards on the breeze to hang motionless before you, eye to eye, a surrealistic instance of cross species contact, but with no comprehension on either side.

At this height, on a clear day, it is possible to see St Kilda on the horizon. Much closer to hand in all directions on the surrounding hill tops and slopes is the evidence of intensive peat digging. Field walls stand proud of the surrounding ground surface because the peat soil on either side of the wall has been dug out. Mingulay could constantly have supported a relatively large resident community, since the food resources have always been there to ensure survival, but fuel for fire is also a necessary requirement. Although the first settlers in the late Mesolithic/early Neolithic most likely found a light woodland of mainly birch, hazel and willow, the demands made upon it for cooking, construction, craft industries and simply warmth would soon have depleted the stocks even if a programme of careful conservation may have been attempted. Peat as a fuel would have been quickly appreciated and to a small extent extraction would be offset by growth. Even this resource would become depleted over time with the growth of population and the added burden of supplying other islands where peat stocks are limited or, as in the case of Berneray, almost non-existent. This situation appears to have become critical by the early modern period when even the Mingulay peat beds are said to have become depleted and all the best material used up. This is when peat dryers may have become necessary, possibly because the poorer quality peat now being dug tended to disintegrate and blow away when left to dry at the cuttings if not contained, and so a surround of crude open stone walling was built. Our survey recorded 120 of these structures on the Mingulay hilltops and high ground where the cuttings were, but none on any of the other islands.

A notable resident population still occupies these high grounds during the breeding season, a population that soon makes itself known if intruded upon. These are the nesting pairs of skua, large powerful birds extremely territorial and willing to defend their domain against all comers, however large. Their high speed, low level attacks may initially appear exciting and fun, but they are in deadly earnest and their passes become ever closer unless deterred in some manner. They have been know to cause death and should not be taken lightly.

Once Mingulay became uninhabited it began to assume the mantle of legend and romance, a mystic place of Gaelic tradition culminating in the composition of songs and poems (the best known being the *Mingulay Boat Song* and *Song to the Isle of Mingulay*). Today Mingulay is the most visited of the uninhabited islands with frequent day trips for tourists from Castlebay and the occasional call by the luxury cruiser *Hebridean Princess*. A dubious honour for any peaceful island.

Next in our northerly journey is the island of Pabbay, an island only slightly larger than Berneray. There is an east-facing valley containing a deserted early modern settlement overlooking a sandy crescent beach and dune system. The sand has plastered the low hills on the northern side along their southern slopes. In many ways this is similar to Mingulay, but all on a much reduced scale. The valley is small and settlement consists of only a few houses and barns. However, by a quirk of nature the crescent beach and dune system are comparable in magnitude to those on Mingulay. The hills of Pabbay are of little significance except for The Hoe in the western corner of the island that boasts a height above sea level of 171m. The general lack of high relief has deprived Pabbay of any spectacular sea cliff scenery and consequently the island does not have large bird colonies like Berneray and Mingulay. The low topography around the bay area has allowed the sand blow from the beach and dunes not just to plaster the lower hillsides, but to pass completely over into the sea on the far side. The vertical division between machair type soils and peat type soils is almost knife edge sharp with the line between them drawn up the hillside against the face of fault line or dyke channel leading from the north-west corner of the valley and is a distinctive visual feature of the bay area.

Excavations in the grass-covered dunes slightly above the valley floor on the north side of the valley revealed a stone structure dating to the Bronze Age set deeply into the sand. The excavations also revealed that the sand in which this 'earth house' had been built was at the same level now as it was in the Bronze Age, indicating that this area of the dune system had been stabilised and remained so since at least that time. This situation of stability, behind the active dunes at the edge of the upper beach, is confirmed by the presence of a Christian cemetery modified from an inland relict dune, now grassed over, but with unnaturally steep, almost vertical sides. The age of this cemetery can be placed in the early Christian period and is notable for the presence of the famous Pabbay Pictish symbol stone. This picture of stability appears to be in contrast with the situation on Mingulay.

Away from the bay area, apart from a large shallow grassy hollow immediately to the west in which can be found the still standing stone-walled corrals used for the ponies that were once bred on the island, the rest of the island appears bleak, wind swept and in large areas denuded of soil and vegetation. This is a slight exaggeration since there are many other small grassy places, nooks and crannies, but the bleakness is there and the archaeology thin on the ground. There is one strange place of note, but not of cheerful remembrance – it is a small enclosed high valley in a central position north-west from the bay area. Several dykes or fault lines meet here and may be the reason for its existence. Being enclosed on all sides it feels dark and the otherwise omnipresent sound of the sea does not penetrate, introducing a feeling of dead air, a heaviness. It is a depressing place where past evil deeds can be imagined, yet it is one of the few locations in all of the islands where some small stunted trees happily grow, protected and sheltered from the west winds.

While occasional trippers may call in at Pabbay, usually to try and find the symbol stone, Sandray, the next island to the north appears to be rarely visited even though it is so much closer to Vatersay, the first of the inhabited islands, and Barra. In the many weeks over the years that we have spent living on Sandray while surveying and excavating we saw no visitors. This is inexplicable, for each of the islands has some special aspect that makes it worthy of attention. Berneray has probably the least to offer, but it is also the furthest and most remote of the islands which does give it a certain amount of mystery. Mingulay has the romantic aura encouraged in song and linked with a large deserted village and importantly it also had a larger population with many local descendants to keep the stories and myths alive.

In this competition of comparative attractions Sandray should be eminently placed, for it was home to some of the legendary Vatersay raiders of 1908, local heroes who became national symbols of the struggle against landlords and the aristocracy for the simple right for a place to live. Their houses still exist in the north-west corner of the island at Sheader, a small hamlet built over, and out of, earlier blackhouses which are themselves perched on top of a tell-like mound of earlier prehistoric sites. Of other interests Sandray is probably the most diverse of the islands in its natural settings and qualities, but they are of a more subtle nature and tend to draw less attention.

Sandray is a blob of an island, 2.5 x 2.7km in diameter, but its rotundity has been modified and deformed by a series of fault lines and dykes, mostly orientated north-east to south-west, which have encouraged clefts and inlets to be eroded to that orientation and allowed the more resistant rock to form headlands in the same direction. This geologically controlled manipulation of the topography, combined with a concentration of the high ground central to the island, notably the hill of Cairn Galtar, 207m, and a coastline of low relief, has allowed the formation of a number of sandy bays at various locations around the coast. A combination of faulting, dykes and persistent erosion have resulted in the carving out of a high pass through the east side of Cairn Galtar hill creating the separate hill of Carnach and one of the unusual features of Sandray – a cliff that faces inland. In the sheltered valleys and clefts inland can be found small clumps of scrub woodland.

On each side of the island, east and west, are two long coastal valleys following the geological pattern. At the head, i.e. north-west corner of the western valley, is a small bay with a beach overlooked by the Sheader settlement. South from the settlement along the valley is a complex of garden plots and enclosures which occupy some of the best arable land on the island. At the southern end of the valley an inland lake, Loch na Cuilce, unique to the southern uninhabited island group, has formed in a depression. The lake receives its waters from the slopes of Cairn Galtar which also collect in a broad shallow depression on the southern coastal plain. Being too shallow to form a true lake this boggy area has become the habitat for a large area of reed which has provided thatching material for the surrounding islands over uncounted years. At the southern end of the valley is another bay with a cobbled beach; a small early modern settlement is also located here.

A great cleft eroded out of the eastern side of Cairn Galtar has formed a rocky prominence, sheer on all sides except for a narrow sloped ridge that allows a restricted approach from the north-east. Perched at the high southern end stands a galleried dun dominating the eastern valley, loch and coastline. It represents, in its original undamaged condition, a statement in stone of power and prestige, an image similar to the early Norman castle keep (**colour plate 6**). Today however it is ruinous and the defences slighted, the walls apparently having been hurled down to provide stone for shelters at the cliff base for itinerant rabbit catchers of the early twentieth century. Degraded and often difficult to immediately recognise, maybe, but the air of Arthurian romance still clings when the grey mists swirl around the remnants that still brood over the landscape.

The valley along the east coast has a similar twin bay and beach arrangement, but only the northern bay has settlement remains, which also include a now missing Christian cemetery of Cille Bhride. The valley, however, is completely different. The east coastline is completely indented so the headlands at each end tend to form breakwaters which have allowed a shell sand beach to evolve. Sand blown from this beach has filled the valley and, especially at the northern end, built up massive dunes against the hillside. A long time ago a huge dune at the back of the beach deflated and a great hole was hollowed out of its centre. In the face of the hole narrow hardened striations of old land stabilisation surfaces can be seen speckled with carbonised wood fragments from past fires. On a wider ledge of an old dune/land surface at one side a mass of stonework, now in disarray, marks some site of unknown, but possibly prehistoric date. From the sea the thin line of the beach with the hollowed out bowl of the dune above and behind have been aptly named the 'wine glass'.

The lack of sea cliffs and hence bird colonies is compensated for by a slightly more varied topography and range of natural habitats. This may account for the less nucleated early modern settlement pattern and the very varied and dispersed pattern of earlier monuments. Eighty per cent of the land surface is composed of rocky terraces and high benches, and with around ten per cent of the ground covered by shell sand dunes the agricultural potential, apart from the west valley, leans towards rough pasture.

The next island to the north of Sandray is Vatersay which is separated by a strip of water so narrow that on a calm day crossing the gap by rowing boat would not be difficult as long as the tide was not running strongly through the Sound. Vatersay is the first of the still inhabited islands in this journey, although until the causeway link to Barra was constructed in the late 1980s there was a distinct danger that Vatersay would join the other southern islands and become deserted. Our modern techno-logical society, even one linked closely to the sea, finds it difficult to survive in a marginal environment without road transport.

Vatersay is dominated by two crescent bays providing over a kilometre and a half of uninterrupted shell sand beach which may claim to be the finest in the whole island chain. Like two duellists they stand back to back almost touching, one facing east and the other facing west, forming a long narrow isthmus. The bay to the west faces the restless, never-ending Atlantic rollers (**colour plate 7**) which have been responsible for a steeply angled beach profile with a storm beach of cobbles thrown to the back of the shell sand beach. In contrast the east facing beach (Vatersay Bay) is not only fronting a more benign sea, but the headlands to the south and more especially to the north are long and sheltering so that the beach is less sloped and there is no higher storm beach. The isthmus between them is a sandwich of two separate dune systems on either side of a central strip of machair. Just 500m separate the two beaches. From above the island it has the appearance of once being shaped like a rounded apple up to 5km in diameter, but through faulting and weak rock forms erosion has eaten through the centre from both sides leaving the shape of a well-chewed apple core. The southern end, 3.5km long and 1km wide, on an east to west axis, is hollowed out enough to form a less impressive shell beach facing Sandray across the sound. Just above the beach are the still standing gable ends and chimneys of a recently deserted hamlet. The landscape at this end is generally gently rounded and smoothed out, having benefited from wind blows forming a machair soil in many places. Vatersay township, a thin scatter of buildings, is located at this southern end of the island.

The rugged northern end is more massive both in area and elevation, 5.5km long by 2km wide, dominated by the elongated hill of Heishival standing almost 200m high with its steep sides and terraces covered in peat soil and heather. To the north of the central hill is a bumpy coastal plain relieved by the small hill of Caolis upon which stands an Iron Age broch. At the eastern end of this most northerly area is the small bay of Cornaig which was the local ferry landing place before the causeway was constructed further along the north coast around Ben Orosay headland. From there a single lane tarmac road leads to the township in the south.

There are no extensive sea cliffs or bird colonies, but a small island, Biruaslam, only separated from the eastern point of the northern half of Vatersay by an eroded sea dyke, has precipitous cliffs on most sides. A wall appears to defend the eastern tip of the island which is reminiscent of the situation at Dun Mingulay although there the peninsula is yet to become finally separated and is still connected by a narrow, much eroded rocky umbilical.

Other tourist attractions are the scattered aluminium remnants of a Catalina flying boat which crashed into the east-facing slope of Heishival in 1944, and a monument set in the dunes of the west bay commemorating the memory of over 400 souls ship-wrecked in the *Annie Jane* on their way to the Americas.

The last island and human focus of the southern islands is Barra (**4**), separated from Vatersay by just 200m of water, the Sound of Vatersay, across which the Vatersay bulls were once forced to swim, towed behind a row boat. Now the two islands are linked by the causeway, a construction which was greeted with mixed feelings on both sides, and has promoted a sometimes heated discussion about a possible similar northern link to South Uist. Barra, the largest of our islands, is a roughly square (7 x 8km) block of land leaning backwards slanted to the north-east with the plumed spur of the Eoligarry peninsula jutting to the north. At the south-west corner the great club foot of Ben Tangaval kicks out. Rising over 300m it rivals Heaval (380m) in dominating the southern half of the island. These two hills are separated by the Tangusdale valley across the angle of the corner which at each end opens into a bay area each with a settlement, Tangusdale to the north and Castlebay, the medieval and modern settlement focus, to the south. Castlebay itself is commanded by Kisimul Castle built on an offshore rocky islet within the bay area. Tangusdale also has a small castle keep built on either a natural knoll or an artificial islet, possibly of prehistoric date, set in a loch that butts against the northern base of Ben Tangaval.

The northern side of the Tangusdale bay area is formed by a broad stub of a flat headland which is a spur out of the Borve valley, the prehistoric settlement focus of the island (**colour plate 8**). North from the headland the coast weaves around several shallow sandy bays where seals can be seen basking out on the wave-washed rocks and sometimes, with patience, heard to sing. Along this coastline, including the Borve headland, the seaward end of its valley and the Tangusdale area, are the machair lands. The eastern coastline is of a totally different nature being rugged and rocky with few sandy inlets, although an excellent harbour can be found at North Bay, along with bays mostly edged by low wave-polished rock as at Brevig.

4   Map of Barra with some of the sites and places mentioned in the text

Castlebay is the gateway to the southern islands with a regular car ferry service from the mainland. Most tourists, once they have visited Kisimul castle, posted their cards from Castlebay post office and perhaps climbed Heaval, head north to one of the most remarkable features of the island, the airstrip at Eoligarry, where the compacted cockle shell beds that floor the eastern bay of Eoligarry provide a runway that is washed twice a day by the sea. At the north end of the island is the small medieval church of Cille Barra where an early Christian Norse cross slab gravestone of a style considered to originate from the Isle of Man can be found. Carved on the reverse side is a Runic inscription which translated reads 'After Thorgerth, Steinar's daughter this cross was raised'. The cross in the church is a resin replica provided by the National Museum who appropriated the original.

The wonders do not stop there because the airstrip in the bay is only the eastern side of a long strip of machair (**colour plate 9**) fronted by an impressive dune system which forms a backdrop to possibly the most magnificent beach in the Western Isles. Its silver shell sand stretches in an unbroken line for over a kilometre and, unbeliev- ably, it is frequently completely deserted. At the northern end of the beach a stiff climb gives access to a cave in which human bones were once recovered, and then higher still the hill is crowned by Dun Scurrival, an Iron Age monument from which views of Eoligarry beach, the bulk of Barra behind to the south and the blue hazed mountains of South Uist to the north are among some of the most memorable.

At Northbay the road from Eoligarry meets the ring-road around the heart of the island, and if you believe the road-sign at the junction, Castlebay is equidistant whichever route is taken, either east or west. Turning west, one passes one of the few areas of true woodland on the island, growing vigorously in a small sheltered cleft at the side of the road, creating a fleeting impression of what the island might have looked like before man and sheep denuded the landscape. Further on, alongside Loch an Duin, a strange quirk of geology has produced a rugged profile of the elderly Queen Victoria.

Barra is full of such sights and scenes whatever the route, but perhaps the most memorable are those that are removed from the road and the convenience of the car. After visiting the archaeology of Alt Chrisal by the Barra end of the Vatersay causeway, leave the car and trek up over the west side of Ben Tangaval and into the green valley of Gortein where the deserted village nestles quietly above its own private little bay and beach. Continue around the hillside and stumble upon the secret valley of Glen Bretadale where the silence can become almost tangible and the signs of humanity reduced to a single small collection of lonely tumbled stone huts. Continue on up over the flank of the hill to the north and find the great monolithic stones of ancient tombs, then climb down off the hillside to discover the Iron Age dun/broch Dun Bán. Similar treks can be made around the Borve valley where a whole range of prehistoric sites are to be found or a walk in the Dark Glen through peat cuttings and by lochs. These are now well-known if demanding routes and are often recommended at the tourist office, but perhaps the most satisfying are those unplanned explorations that stumble upon the less well known. There are many secret little valleys such as Crubisdale hidden in the hills behind the Nask settlement at Castlebay. Boats were once built here and pushed nearly a kilometre to the sea. On Barra alone there is enough archaeology, island history (there are two small museums), natural history, peace and quiet, walking, beachcombing, fishing, sailing, and cycling – not to mention the festivals, music and highland games – to warrant more than a single visit.

To the islanders the summer tourists may appear to flood the islands, but if global warming continues that flood may become a deluge as whole populations move north away from growing deserts. This would almost bring us full circle for the islands were born out of the last global warming that heralded the end of the Ice Age. The islands awoke emerging from under the ice sheet to become clothed in birch and hazel and to become the furthest margin of north–west Europe. Populations also moved north then into this remote and marginal landscape, but only as trickle rather than a flood.

2 Marginal landscapes

During the last Ice Age the Hebridean long island, apart from the peaks of its mountain chain, was hidden and depressed like the rest of Scotland under a thick mantle of ice. When the ice finally retreated, exposing the land once more, the region would have become available, possibly for the very first time, for human exploitation. Who were the first people to set foot in the Outer Hebrides and when did they arrive? These are two of the most tantalising questions in Scottish prehistory today and many an archaeologist would like to be the first to answer them. At present there is no firm archaeological evidence for the presence of Mesolithic hunter-gatherer communities existing or seasonally visiting the Outer Isles, even though over a decade of intensive archaeological research has been focused on the area. On the other hand the pollen records for several sites on Barra and South Uist provide just a glimmer of a possibility that there was some human activity during this early period. They have also provided a much clearer description of the post-glacial island landscape in which any early colonist would have lived.

The pollen diagrams show the late glacial to Holocene transition taking place some 10,000 years ago with the arrival and rapid expansion of birch later followed by hazel; thereafter lesser numbers of elm and oak begin to colonise. The landscape appears to have been well wooded, although many treeless areas, especially along the exposed western seaboard, still persisted. At around 6000 BC, according to many of the pollen diagrams, there was a marked decline in birch and hazel, which corresponds to an appearance of significant amounts of microscopic charcoal fragments in the samples. At present this combination is considered to reflect some human impact on the environment, with Mesolithic hunter-gatherers probably using underwood and felled trees for domestic campfires rather than deliberate forest clearance for game control. Archaeologists in general accept the environmental specialists' view, explaining the apparent lack of artefacts and 'sites' as being due to a combination of post-glacial isostatic movements drowning coastal lowlands, especially to the west, and to the steady growth of peat deposits covering much of the inland landscape. Discovery of the Mesolithic may depend, therefore, more on some lucky chance find rather than an organised and specific research project.

Then there is the question of how rapid the human colonisation would have been. With the amelioration of climatic conditions huge areas of landscape in the north once again became available. Wild game would have become abundant in a diverse range of new environments and the coastal areas would have been exceptionally rich in a wide variety of food products. There is however a crucial gap in our knowledge that has considerable bearing upon any attempted reconstruction of the Mesolithic, and that is the size of the population in the regions. Most archaeologists would agree that the population at any time during the Scottish Mesolithic was numerically low. However it is possible to imagine the west coast of Scotland and its emerging inner islands as being rapidly encompassed within the sphere of human activity by pioneer bands. With such a massive area of high potential becoming available, even with a higher population than is perhaps at present envisaged for the period, would the early colonists need, or even feel the urge, to cross the intervening waters to reach the 'long island'? The gain in resources would not have been any great increase on those more readily available on the mainland and inner islands and, in fact, with the absence of large game animals, may actually have been less.

Some large land mammals may have been able to quickly colonise the western fringe of the Scottish mainland as the ice sheets retreated, but if the inundation of the deep Minch trench by the meltwaters and rising sea levels was rapid, then the 'long island' would have become isolated from the rest of western Scotland effectively preventing the migration of such animals. Any Mesolithic hunter would have found little large game to hunt, but it is probable that some groups did eventually colonise and it is feasible that they brought with them a breeding stock of deer, since it is quite likely that they had a far better management of their 'wild stock' than is appreciated today. Without direct evidence it is difficult to say more than this, but a small amount of deer bone and antler has been found in later Neolithic assemblages at least proving the presence of deer early in the prehistoric period.

Modern archaeology is still haunted by its own precepts that were formulated during its early development. The regulation and ordering of time, social and technological innovations, and environmental stages became one of the keystones to mastering the data that was being accumulated, and from it the great periodic ages of mankind were written into the history books. Such schemes can be difficult to erase or modify after a time, but it is now generally realised that the classic archaeological divisions, while still being of some value, should not be considered geographically and chronologically rigid. The change from hunting and gathering to farming, from Mesolithic to Neolithic, with all the social and technological adjustments, did not happen instantly and did not happen uniformly. For example, around the coast of northern Europe from Denmark to Finland and Norway it is now known that communities of the Ertebolle culture remained in a Mesolithic state while their contemporaries further inland took on the trappings and burdens of the Neolithic and became farmers. The reason for this anomaly appears to relate to the rich seafood resources of a stable marine environment in the coastal regions which allowed the Ertebolle to resist the much more risky agricultural way of life that was being embraced by their inland neighbours. Certain benefits, however, were not ignored. Pottery, for example, that symbol and distinctive element used to define the Neolithic, was assimilated and has been found on a number of these late Mesolithic sites. Farming was only embraced when the Ertebolle lost their rich shellfish beds to rising sea levels.

A similar situation occurred in the Western Isles with rising sea levels gradually drowning the coastal lowlands. However, unlike the Ertebolle, the island communities would not have been subjected to significant stresses on their resources. The rich seafood breeding grounds were merely transferred to the inundated coastal lowlands. Always a marginal environment at the north-western edge of Europe, cursed with a climate producing severe gales, short summers and long winters, the islands offered little encouragement for the development of arable farming. One of its prerequisite conditions, however, may have been adopted already. By the late Mesolithic a sedentary way of life may have already become accepted due to the increasingly restricted island space creating a tendency towards the formation of settled communities based primarily on fishing.

The whole concept of the Neolithic, with its multi-level transformations which fundamentally affected a wide spectrum of human consciousness, social, economic and technological, may have been promoted in this region more by religious motivations than as a practical alternative lifestyle. Little credence is now given to the idea of waves of European Neolithic agriculturists complete with ploughs, bags of seeds and herds of domestic animals migrating into the north, and to consider such a mass migration all the way into the outer isles is even less believable. The assimilation of the Mesolithic communities into the Neolithic way of life, especially in the far north-west, may therefore have been slow and patchy. Many people may not have changed their way of life at all, only accepting those things that they regarded as significant or worthy.

In fact evidence of any kind for the Neolithic is not abundant. Almost all of the known sites are ritual monuments with only isolated examples of proven domestic settlements. This however is not an unusual feature of the period; it is a condition that is replicated, especially throughout lowland Britain, due mainly to the almost exclusive use of timber for domestic structures and a generally greater use of stone for the ritual. There is naturally a notable exception, the Northern Isles, where the native fissile rock type almost begs to be used not only for houses, but even for the furniture within them, a fortuitous circumstance in a landscape with few natural timber resources. Unlike the Northern Isles, the Hebrides do not have such obliging bedrock but, as we shall see, the evident shortage of suitable timber did to some extent encourage the use of stone for domestic architecture.

Our knowledge of the Neolithic settlement of the southern islands would be almost entirely based upon funerary and ritual monuments if not for a fortuitous set of circumstances that led the Sheffield University research team to excavate a late eighteenth-century homestead at Alt Chrisal on the southern coastline of Barra. A large blackhouse had been constructed upon a neatly finished stone-faced platform built against the southern hillslope and set back into the shelter of the narrow Alt Chrisal glen. Along the back of the house a drainage ditch had been cut and it was the excavation of this ditch that revealed the presence of a much earlier prehistoric site. A series of excavations from 1989 to 1994 on the platform and the other associated buildings slowly exposed a domestic Neolithic settlement complex. A calibrated C14 date of 3600 BC was gained from charcoal considered to be in a context secondary only to the primary deposits and structures.

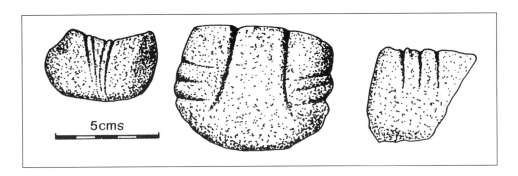

5   *Neolithic net-floats of pumice from Alt Chrisal. The pumice floated across the Atlantic from Iceland; it appears to have been tied to the nets with twine or sinews which have left their mark on the soft material*

A section cut down through the front of the platform beneath the blackhouse revealed that the neat stone revetment was an eighteenth-century encasement of an earlier Neolithic structure (T26). The original Neolithic platform was a much cruder construction of large stones piled between and linking natural boulders lying on the hillside to form a revetment, approximately 14m long, behind which earth and stone was packed and levelled.

The blackhouse occupies and obscures the front 12m of the platform, but fortunately the Neolithic occupation extends 3m further back into the hillside. Unfortunately the blackhouse builders appear to have reused most of the exposed Neolithic stonework, hence our inability, during the initial excavations of the blackhouse, to recognise the few apparently randomly exposed stones on the surface behind the house as being an earlier site. Limited excavations within the blackhouse and to a greater extent in the open area behind the house showed the primary Neolithic occupation (Phases 1 and 2) to be characterised by post settings, small fire settings, shallow gullies cut in a series of arcs, and a small amount of apparently displaced stonework. Our interpretation of these structures and deposits may change radically in the future, especially if further excavations are carried out on portions of the site that were left unexcavated, but at present the foundation of the site appears to indicate a considerable investment in time and labour. Although comparatively crude in construction, the platform is substantial, suggesting a planned long-term occupancy. The location in a coastal area removed from the better agricultural land would indicate a type of fishing/herding economy envisaged for the sedentary late Mesolithic coastal communities suggested above. This is reinforced by the discovery in the excavations of sea-borne Icelandic volcanic pumice distinctively grooved to act as fishing net floats (**5**). Carbonised grain from the primary deposits of Alt Chrisal show that, as elsewhere during Hebridean Neolithic, the only cereal crop grown was six-row barley, although small quantities of blackberries, strawberries and hazelnuts were gathered to supplement the diet. Weed seeds generally connected with cultivation were also

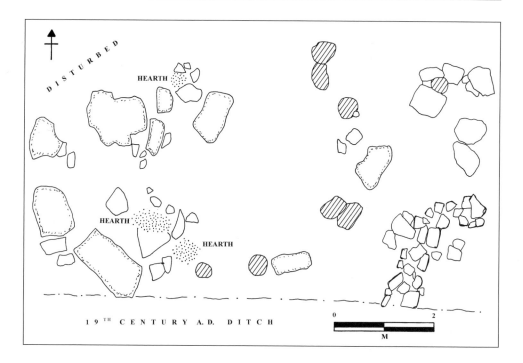

HEARTH

DISTURBED

HEARTH

HEARTH

19 TH CENTURY A. D. DITCH

0   2

M

6 *Early Neolithic occupation area at Alt Chrisal, Barra, in phase 1B. The arc of shaded post-pits may have belonged to a timber-framed structure with other posts erected on the stone blocks to the left; the wall foundation at bottom right probably supported a turf superstructure. A C14 date of around 3600 BC was obtained for the small hearth near the top of the figure.*

found, all of which may indicate that small-scale cultivation took place in the settlement environs, although it may also be possible that they derived from supplies traded from other communities with access to better soils.

As revealed by the excavations, the structures and deposits on the platform were of an apparently ephemeral nature, which is often accepted as the normal situation for sites of this period. In reality we envisage that these remains represent a far from insubstantial, low roundhouse or sub-circular house, with solid external load bearing walls, composed mainly of turf, possibly laid on stone footings, and with extensive use of timber supports internally. In the earliest phase (**6**) a number of post pads and post pits indicate that suitable timber was available for construction work at this time and was possibly used for the roof supports or for internal partitions. Several gully arcs indicate a ground plan of some circularity, but remnant displaced stone work, which may have been extensively robbed for later phases of construction, is too sparse and incoherent to form a sensible structural picture. Hearths in the form of charcoal-filled hollows and areas of baked soil are evident in both Phase 1 and Phase 2 but, in the later phase, there is the addition of a large rectangular stone-lined oven or fireplace (**colour plate 10**). In a wide area around

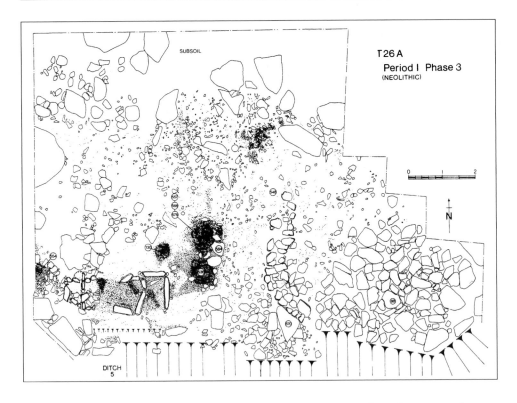

SUBSOIL

T26 A

Period I Phase 3
(NEOLITHIC)

N

DITCH
5

7   *The Later Neolithic occupation at Alt Chrisal, in phase 3. At the right is a paved area*
   ('the patio'), flanked to the west by a curving wall foundation. At the bottom left is a
   large stone-edged hearth, and close by the remains of clamps where pottery was fired.
   One of these gave a C14 date of around 2700 BC

the main stone hearth, presumably the living floor area, deep laminated deposits of
ash and burnt soil accumulated and appear to have merged without interruption
into similar deposits found in Phase 3.

In Phase 3 (**7**) considerable changes occurred. Stone in general was in greater
evidence and a large area of paving was laid in the south-eastern corner of the
exposed area at this time. Wall footings may be represented by a single linear
spread, but no other associated footings were found which would form some
coherent structure. If they existed they appear to have been either robbed out or
obscured under the blackhouse. A large rectangular hearth with two compart-
ments edged in stone slightly overlay the oven/hearth found in Phase 2, for which
it may have been a direct replacement as the accumulated peat ash overwhelmed
the earlier structure. Just to the east of the hearth were two thick deposits, circular
in plan, of concentrated charcoal, burnt soil and ash in which some evidence of
blocks of peat remain. Our interpretation of one of these peat deposits is that it is
possibly the remains of a small clamp kiln for firing pottery. This is suggested in
the context of normal domestic needs and not in the form of an intensive craft

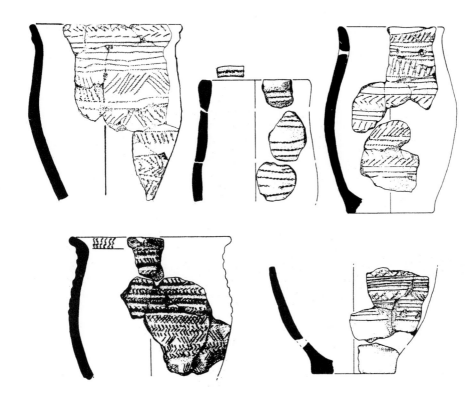

8   A selection of beakers from Late Neolithic Alt Chrisal. About 35 examples could be identified, with decoration made by cord, bone and shell impressions and incision. After A. Gibson

workshop production centre. A C14 date from the material suggests the clamp was in use around 2700BC.

During the final phase (Phase 4) considerable rebuilding took place with the construction of a substantial roundhouse, approximately 6m in diameter, defined by what appears to be the northern half of a circular inner wall stone revetment, most likely for a turf superstructure. The entrance and a possible porch of large stones set on edge were located to the east opening out onto the still-used stone paving of the previous Phase 3. The eighteenth-century blackhouse and ditch effectively eliminate any sign of the southern return of the wall circuit. A small cist was annexed to the outside of the north wall and the western end of the wall arc was extended to form another possible small annex. Within the internal area of the house in the north-eastern quadrant, immediately to the side of the eastern entrance, a mass of stonework may represent some form of raised bed platform. There were also several small hearths and a large pad of stone set off-centre towards the southern side which may have supported a roof post. However, it is impossible to be certain of the structural details when so much may have been disturbed or robbed later.

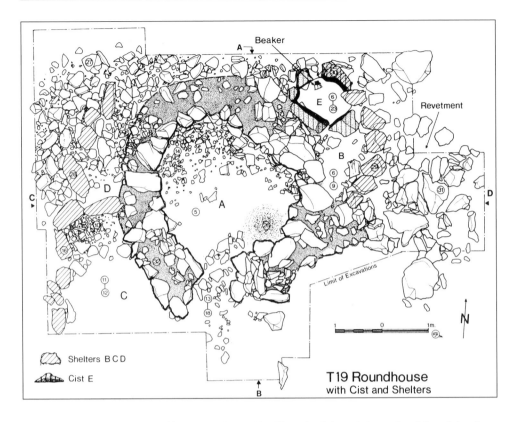

9 *Plan of the Beaker roundhouse at T19, Alt Chrisal. A hearth is to the right of the door, and the storage cist to the rear. The floor was heavily worn down, and floor sweepings with flints and pottery were found scattered down the slope outside the door*

During Phase 4 or the end of Phase 3 the settlement expanded, with several other structures, a substantial roundhouse (T19) and small hut (T18), being built further up the glen to the north, while across the Alt Chrisal stream to the west a further small hut (T15) was also possibly built at this time. This phase is dated to the end of the Neolithic period with its transition into the early Bronze Age in the late third millennium BC and is recognised by the appearance of a new, highly decorated type of pottery vessel – the beaker.

Beaker pottery is commonly in the form of a drinking vessel with the decoration, often covering the whole vessel, usually in horizontal bands filled with patterns formed by the extensive use of impressions made with twisted cord and fine toothed combs (**colour plate 11**). These vessels are commonly found placed in burials of the period, but as the numerous sherds mixed in with the other domestic wares at Alt Chrisal indicate, they were also used domestically (**8**). The sudden appearance of these highly decorated vessels on sites at the end of the Neolithic period prompted many archaeologists to consider the possibility of an invasion by people from Europe. Certainly, all over Britain, there were profound changes both in social relationships

10 *A complete beaker as found in the cist at roundhouse T19, Alt Chrisal. Although com-plete beakers found in cists are normally associated with burials, the cist in this case may have been a domestic 'cold-box'*

and perceptions as well as in the material culture of the population. Burial practices changed radically, focusing upon the individual in individual graves rather than the community in communal tombs for example, but it is now generally accepted that this was an invasion of socio-religious concepts rather than actual people.

The roundhouse T19 (**colour plate 12**) is an important addition to the list of Neolithic houses because, apart from its reuse as a sheiling in more modern times and the usual natural amount of erosion, it has suffered less damage and modifi-cation than most of the other prehistoric buildings on the site. The construction (**9**) as it survives is of a metre-thick stone-faced wall encasing an earthen core with an internal diameter of 3m. The external wall face is only evident at the sides of the south-facing doorway. The missing stonework was most likely robbed out to build the sheiling shelters. If further erosion and displacement was to occur then the result could be similar to the situation found on the platform with just one of the stone wall faces forming an arc. Also comparable to T26, although on a smaller scale, is the piled stone platform of T19 that was built into the hillside to provide a level surface; both houses also have a small annex or cist attached to the northern outer wall. In the T19 annex a complete Beaker vessel (**10**) was found, and while it is always tempting to find a ritual significance in such a discovery, labelling them 'placed objects', it may in reality be little more than a forgotten or misplaced article. If a ritual significance is sought then it may be as a domestic material culture object of the household deliberately placed to signify the abandonment of the site.

A similar possible ritually placed object, a half-complete bowl in a distinctive form known as Unstan ware, was found placed below a large post hole packing stone (567) of the Phase 1a period of T26. If the same reasoning is applied then this must surely be a ritually placed object signifying the founding of the settlement.

All the Neolithic structures of the settlement built after the primary phase appear to have been constructed with free-standing stone and earth walls as the main load-bearing element. Post pits were totally absent, even those required for room partitioning, for by this time – possibly due to grazing by sheep and the continual depletion of the timber reserves for domestic fires and light craft industries – the islands had become largely deforested. All of the buildings, whatever their mode of construction, were substantial; it is difficult to imagine an insubstantial building surviving for long in the Hebrides. Many Neolithic sites may appear to consist of insubstantial huts with associated spreads of ash, hearths and post holes but, with the extensive use of cut turf blocks for building, a substantial weather-proof superstructure can be attained which leaves little evidence. We hope that the excavations at Alt Chrisal will help to dispel any idea that the domestic sites of the Hebridean Neolithic were necessarily flimsy and ephemeral.

Several finds from the excavations – fragments of bloodstone from the island of Rum, pitchstone from Arran and polished stone axes from Northern Ireland – give some indication that, although the islands are on the margin of Neolithic Europe, they still managed occasional contacts with some parts of the north-western seaboard from Northern Ireland and up along the Argyll coast. This view is reinforced by the presence of pottery forms and decorative styles popular in the islands to the north as far as the Northern Isles where the Unstan type of bowl is thought to originate.

In general the pottery and stonework found on the site also allow us a glimpse from which to judge the level of technology in everyday use. The possible presence of small pottery clamps or bonfire kilns has already been noted and the large assemblage of locally produced ceramics clearly shows the potting skills achieved, not only the fineness attained in some of the fabrics and firing, but also in the wide range of forms and decorative motifs identified with the Hebridean Neolithic (**11**). The larger, sturdy storage jars with rounded bases, plain or everted rims, and sometimes lugs around the waist, were mostly undecorated. Smaller bowls on the other hand were either decorated over their entire surface or had a broad band of decoration below the rim often enclosed by a cordon around the belly of the pot. Using a rich mixture of incised and grooved lines, the impressions of cockle and scallop shells, twisted cord, and even fingernails, the potters produced a remarkable variety of designs. Herringbone, multiple chevrons, alternating panels of vertical and horizontal lines, diagonally hatched triangles, and other motifs are all used liberally; and, as we have seen, towards the end of the period Beaker pottery is introduced.

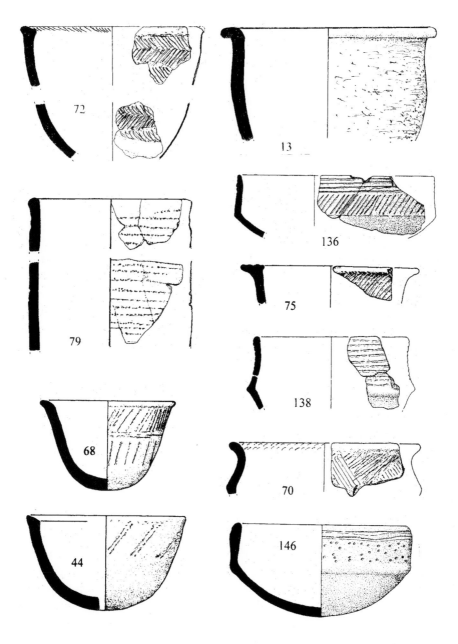

11 A selection of neolithic pottery vessels from Alt Chrisal. Much of the pottery was decorated by impression or incision. Some of the bowls were finely made and decorated, and in some cases (136, 146) can be linked to similar types in Orkney. After A. Gibson

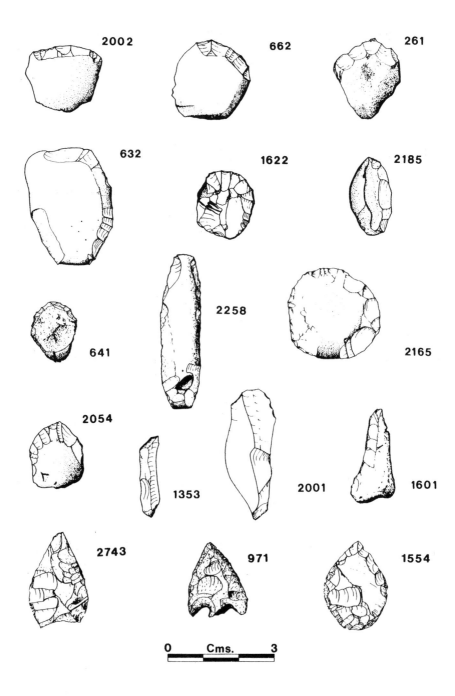

12 Flint tools made from pebble-flint, Alt Chrisal. With flint beach pebbles, rarely more than 2in long, providing the only source of flint, the tool kit was unavoidably miniaturised! After Wickham-Jones

Similar skills and ingenuity are revealed in the production of flint tools. The rocks of the islands' Lewisian Gniess are not suitable for making chipped stone implements, and flint-bearing clays very rarely survived post-glacial erosion. The only source of flint on the islands are the occasional small pebbles washed up on the beaches from deposits on the sea bed. From this unpromising material the island communities managed to create a reasonably wide range of tools, albeit with a decidedly 'miniaturised' look to them (**12**). At Alt Chrisal we found a variety of scrapers, multi-purpose blades, awls and arrowheads, along with a considerable amount of the debris created during manufacture. The distribution of both manufacturing debris and finished articles, within the limits of our exca-vations, tells us something about the use of lithics in and around the homestead – where tools were made and where they were used – and from this we can determine something of the activities and rituals of daily life. The lithics from the roundhouse at T19 were mostly used tools with an above-average number of small retouching flakes suggesting that the activities here were concerned with tool use and maintenance rather than tool production. At the southern limit of the site, around a large boulder on the foreshore, a large collection of lithic material, mainly of flint but with a few items of coarse stone and Rum bloodstone, was composed almost entirely of production debitage. In contrast on and around the main focus of the settlement, the platform and structures of T26, the lithics are more evenly divided between finished articles and manufacturing debitage. Scrapers are particularly common in this assemblage which, along with the several worn fragments of pumice stone, were probably used for the cleansing and prepa-ration of food, such as de-scaling fish, and removing skins, whether from cattle, sheep or seal. In conjunction with these activities the platform also yielded many beach cobbles with wear patterns showing that they had been used for grinding, pounding and polishing.

The acid peat soils have deprived us of most of the products produced by these activities along with any evidence for carpentry, weaving and basketry, all skills important to the survival and well-being of the community. Perhaps our greatest loss to the acid soil is bone, which probably became one of the most useful materials in a landscape that offers so little diversity in resources. Without the discarded animal bone we also lack one of the prime means of investigating the daily diet and agricultural strategy of the community living at Alt Chrisal. However, from the distribution of the inorganic finds that do survive we can learn something of the spatial patterning which reflects the activities of everyday life taking place around the settlement.

There is little doubt that the main focus of the Alt Chrisal settlement in almost every respect is the platform T26. Here the site was founded with the construction of the platform and the timber structures on it. Later large stone-built hearths, always the focus of prehistoric homes, were built, but there were also many other small open hearths, some of which may have been for baking pottery. At the same time the occupants were engaged in a number of other activities related to manufacturing and processing. Flint pebbles were being reduced to make tools, barley was being processed and prepared for food and possibly beer. The scene was no doubt a hive of activity at these times. Towards the end of the period an impressive stone patio was laid outside the east-facing entrance, and while the activities at T26 may have continued unabated, the settlement as a whole expanded with other houses and store huts being constructed.

We considered that the site was inhabited by a single family unit and so perhaps the expansion could be the extension of the kinship group with younger families outgrowing the parental domain. The evidence from the new house T19 is markedly different from that found on the platform. There is little or no sign of manufacturing in any medium. The interior of T19 can boast only a small open hearth with almost a minimal amount of peat ash present. However this is not an indication of short-term usage since the spill of material downslope from the south-facing entrance and the apparent hollowing of the internal floor area both indicate that this house may have been regularly swept clean. There is a distinct impression that some chores were being undertaken by the occupants, the occasional sharpening of a tool for example, but that many of the main events of the day, the family as a whole eating and working, were still part of the life at the main house on the platform below.

In terms of chronology, the radiocarbon dates show the early start of the Neolithic occupation, but it is the ceramics that give the clearest picture of the fullness of the occupation to its termination in the late third millennium BC. Analysis of the 6800 sherds of pottery – representing a minimum of 600 vessels with identifiable rims or decorative motifs, and a further maximum of 388 vessels identified from undecorated sherds on the basis of fabric, form and finish – indicate that the platform appears to have been intensively used throughout the Neolithic. Undecorated bowls, partnered with Hebridean incised wares and, to a lesser extent, Unstan and Impressed wares appeared in all of the excavated Neolithic contexts. Only in the final Neolithic/early Bronze Age did the ceramic repertoire change with the appearance of Beaker pottery, heralding the abandonment of the glen some time in the late third millennium BC. The combination of C14 dates and ceramic analysis therefore suggests that the slightly bucolic description above of the life and times of a Neolithic fisher/farming community may therefore be set in context with a long and apparently peaceful period lasting for well over a millennium.

The sites at Alt Chrisal have been discussed at length, but their unique status as the only example of an extensively excavated Neolithic domestic settlement in the southern islands deserves attention. Although the evidence for other domestic sites is very limited – pottery sherds from a midden deposit at Biruaslum, Vatersay (**13**), and sherds with a stone axe from pits and associated hearth excavated at Balnabodach, Barra – it is no true reflection of reality since the relatively abundant burial and ritual monuments were clearly produced by a sizeable population. The lack of visible domestic sites is undoubtedly due to three factors. Firstly, they were the earliest settlements of substance in the landscape and therefore have a history of continuous stone-robbing and abuse. Secondly, they are likely to be found at preferred site locations, which were reused repeatedly over the millenia, often being submerged or totally obliterated by the later settlement. Thirdly, it is almost impossible to date many sites by field survey alone. There were many small, but substantially built, simple

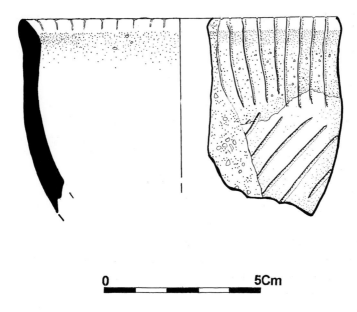

13 A decorated neolithic bowl from an eroding midden on the rocky islet of Biruaslum, Vatersay

roundhouses discovered in the general survey of the islands but, like T19, they were initially thought of as being Iron Age or medieval in date. In the light of experience gained over the years of survey and excavation in the islands a wary confidence has developed and it is now thought that some of the smaller roundhouses are Neolithic and Bronze Age while Iron Age settlement is concentrated in larger and more complex roundhouse types.

On a few Neolithic sites excavated on the Uists organic materials have survived and these provide a link that enables us to more firmly reconstruct the Hebridean Neolithic economy. Of especial importance is the islet site of Eilean Domhnuill where a large proportion of the site has been permanently waterlogged preserving the organic structural elements as well as domestic refuse, even including lengths of rope. The animal bones from this site and the site at Northton situated on the machair, in which bone is also well preserved, show us that sheep similar to the Mouflon was the dominant domestic species, with cattle second. Domestic dogs were common enough, but pig appears with some rarity.

Until the number of domestic Neolithic sites in the southern islands can be counted on more than one hand we have to look to the funerary and ritual monuments to help us in ordering the landscape and accounting for the population. As a small microcosm of Neolithic life the Alt Chrisal settlement again provides a starting point. Such a long-lived settlement must have its sacred element and close to hand on a wide rock shelf 135m OD, high above and out of sight of the settlement, is a circular, 7m diameter, flat cairn with a substantial raised kerb (T214) (**colour plate 13**). On the south-eastern side the kerb turns inwards

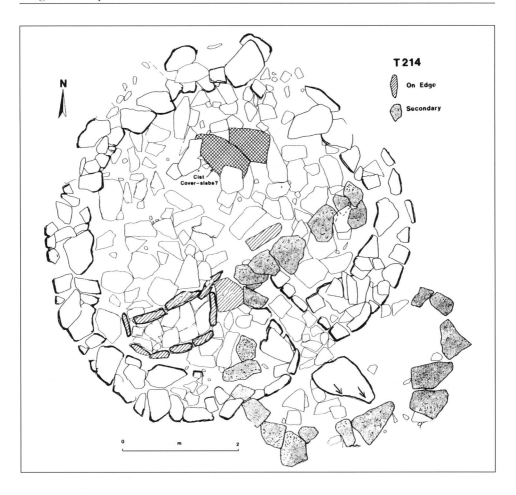

14 Plan of the paved or flat cairn T214, above Alt Chrisal. A cist was found to one side of the inturned entrance, with an upright stone block set at one end. The two cover slabs were found 2m to the north, suggesting the cist may have looted of any contents long ago

forming a flattened indent from which a passage leads into the heart of the cairn. At the entrance to the passage, which points to the south-east, is a fallen 1m long facade or blocking stone (**14**). The internal structuring is confused and most likely shows more than one phase of reconstruction or adaptation. Two slabs set on edge at right-angles to and on opposite sides of the passage at its internal end may be some remains of an original entrance to a central chamber. At the north-east corner of the central area, two large slabs most likely capped that chamber. In this form the cairn is architecturally somewhere between the earlier megalithic passage graves and Bronze Age kerbed cairns. Whether it occupies a similar position chronologically – in the late Neolithic/early Bronze Age – is uncertain. A well-defined rectangular cist, made from vertically set slabs, is set in the south-western quadrant of the cairn. This cist, which could conceivably have originally been a

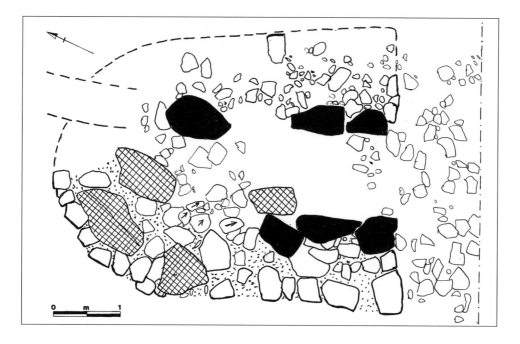

15 Plan of a small wedge- or heel-shaped passage grave T55. The structure had suffered from being incorporated into a nineteenth-century enclosure and adapted to serve as a lambing pen. Six chamber stones still stood upright (black) and four were found toppled (hatched). The structure is typologically somewhere between the Irish wedge-shaped and the Shetland heel-shaped cairns

side chamber leading off the central passage, may be an Early Bronze Age adaptation belonging to the final phase of the early Alt Chrisal settlement.

A possible chambered cairn (T55) could also be associated with the farmstead, although it is 450m along the coast to the east of the Alt Chrisal settlement. Around its megalithic chamber of orthostats (some standing 1m high) there is an apparent elongated heel-shaped cairn (**15**). This monument may have affinities with both Irish 'wedge-shaped' tombs of the late Neolithic and to Shetland heeled-cairns, and in this respect it appears to be a local adaptation of one or the other. The discovery of a second small cairn at Grean on Barra, with a very clear D-shaped cairn and flat, stone facade, strengthens the possibility of a Northern Isles connection for this tomb appears to be a typical heeled-cairn of a type primarily known only from the Shetlands.

Considering the limitations of the locality, Alt Chrisal cannot be considered a major settlement of the kind that might exist in a more preferred settlement area with better soils. Although such settlements may not be easily recognisable, being masked by later buildings, the burial monuments related to such large sites are normally very visible. Such an area is the broad Borve valley in Barra which, although located on the west side of the island and exposed to the westerly gales, does possess some of the best pasture land and an extensive area of machair.

No Neolithic settlements are visible, but field walls buried up to a metre below the peat in the valley floor have been observed in drainage channels. They give some indication of the ease with which ancient landscapes with their fields and settlements can lie hidden out of sight by the thick deposits of blanket peat. Yet one does not have to look far to find the burial monuments that served the first farmers. They are located high on the valley sides, above the agricultural fields, easily seen from the settlement areas below.

The Borve valley has two large passage graves, Dun Bharpa (*c*.30m diameter) and Balnacraig (*c*.25m diameter). The chambers have been opened and probably had their contents removed in antiquity. In fact the Balnacraig tomb has been robbed of its cairn material and many of its larger structural elements have been reused several times over to form other structures dating from as early as the Iron Age and finishing with modern sheilings. Dun Bharpa on the other hand still retains most of its cairn material and even though much material has no doubt been removed to build the nearby modern field walls, it still stands to over 5m high (**colour plate 14**). All of its major megalithic structural elements are present although perhaps slightly displaced. These consist of 15 orthostats measuring around 1m in width and standing up to 4m high, set at intervals around the perimeter of the mound. Additionally the tops of vertically set stone slabs forming the passage to the inner chamber and the roof slabs of that chamber can clearly be seen where the cairn material has been removed, no doubt to gain a plunderer's entrance. The entrance to the passage is set just to the south of east.

Without the skeletal material it is difficult to speculate upon the physical char-acteristics of the resident population. However, it is almost certain that the tombs would have contained an assemblage of bones and artefacts similar to those found in the comparable tombs of the Northern Isles. Such tombs appear to have been used as communal burial houses or sepulchres throughout most of the Neolithic period. The area in front of the passage opening (where the cairn perimeter is commonly indented) usually contains evidence for a variety of activities which most likely took the form of communal rituals. Hearths and spread areas of burnt soil along with animal bone and artefacts, possibly denoting episodic feasting, are often found along with fragments of quartz – a material thought to possess magic qualities – frequently found in and around ritual sites. The narrow passage allows room for just a few individuals to gain access into the interior of the chamber. This restricted access may itself have been a way of creating social and hierarchical divisions – the general community attending at the forecourt, but only the select few allowed admission to the tomb. Inside the chamber the deceased individual's bones ultimately become mixed with the remains of the earlier generations who represented a general pantheon of ancestors rather than identifiable personalities. In some cases the corpses may even have been exposed and de-fleshed before final deposition within the tomb. From finds of Beaker pottery in late contexts, it seems that these tombs became redundant in the final Neolithic/early Bronze Age period after which burial rituals focused on individual burial under small round barrows and cairns.

Even with the evidence from undisturbed tombs in regions where bone preservation is good, such as Quanterness in Orkney, it is difficult to estimate population density. The excavator calculated that the Quanterness tomb contained a possible total of nearly 400 adult burials during the millennium-long lifetime of the monument and that the average adult population of the community was 20 individuals. However, such calculations do at least provide a valuable yardstick and help to put the less well preserved Hebridean data into some form of comparable context. If the two passage graves of the Borve valley, Dun Bharpa and Balnagraig, are considered to have been in use at broadly the same time as the burial monuments of two separate communities occupying the valley then a population of around 40 to 50 adults at any one time may be considered feasible.

On firmer ground, the Quanterness osteological data does provide an indication of the average life expectancy and the physical condition of the Neolithic people in the Northern Isles. Very few individuals survived into old age, the average age at death being approximately 20 years, which is unusually young even for a primitive society. In contrast, the physical characteristics of stature and muscular development are close to the present-day norm and, if one assumes similar lifestyles between the Northern and Western Isles at that time, then the average Neolithic Hebridean is likely to have been only a few inches shorter than people today.

Probably the greatest impression is delivered, not by the analytical detail of the tomb contents, but by the visual impact of the stones themselves, of which the Borve valley passage graves provide two alternative views. The Balnacraig tomb has been dismembered to provide the material for later field walls, shielings and houses, leaving behind a stone carcass of dinosaurian proportions in the form of megalithic orthostats that once formed part of the chamber and entrance passage. Dun Bharpa on the other hand still retains a large proportion of its original cairn clothing the megalithic interior. Whereas Balnacraig presents the stark image of clean picked bones, Dun Bharpa has the form of a still fully fleshed grey hump from a stranded whale, but of fantastic proportions. However dramatic or poetic the descriptions, the message is clear in both cases: a massive input of time and labour has been expended by a community in non-productive activities. The sheer size of the orthostats used in the important structural elements far outstrips the stone blocks used in everyday domestic building and the amount of field stone collected and transported to the cairn site is staggering. How can one interpret the diversion of so much of the community's energy away from the daily effort of subsistence survival? Is this a majestic attempt to penetrate the metaphysical veil that shrouds the meaning of our existence or is it a cowering superstition against forces too immense to contemplate? The answer may be found to lie between these two extremes if one balances the mystic symbolism encoded in the engraved stones of the passage grave at Newgrange in Ireland against the mathematical and astronomical ability illustrated in the late Neolithic standing stones of Callanish.

Outside the Borve valley there are numerous monuments that are most likely chamber tombs, but they are all much smaller than those in the valley and are a

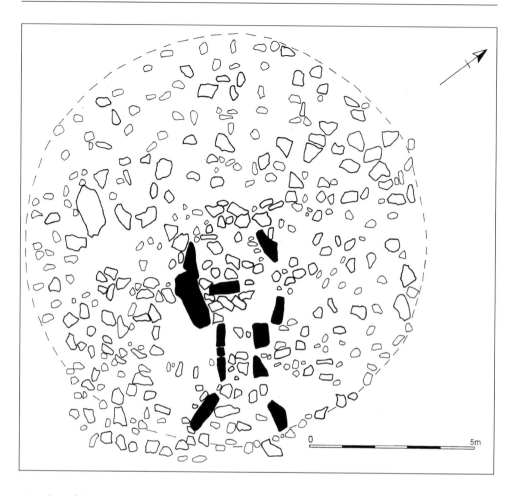

16 Plan of the passage grave on Ben Orosay, Vatersay. Its circular cairn, V-shaped entrance, short passage and small sub-circular chamber are similar to tombs in Uist and Skye

clear indication that Borve was potentially the Neolithic settlement focus of the southern islands. Also the communities outside the valley were probably of much smaller populations, possibly only single family kinship groups. At Cornaig Bay, north Vatersay, only 100m from the seashore and 20m OD, a fine example of a passage grave sits proudly on the spot it has occupied for more than 4000 years. When we found it in June 1989 we could scarcely believe it had never been recorded before. Most of its cairn has been carried away to build walls, and the capping stones of its chamber have disappeared, but the V-shaped entrance, the short passage, and the burial chamber itself are all clearly visible (**16**). This tomb (VN 157) is a close relative of similar tombs found on North and South Uist.

Another chamber tomb (MY 347), at Skipisdale, Mingulay, similarly sited close to the foreshore, was partially excavated but it too was empty and robbed of its stonework. Two further possible tombs were located during the survey of Sandray, one a less than convincing monument on the north-west coast and the other one at the back of the central southern valley. Pabbay has no tombs, but sand-dune formations in the north bay area, a likely location, are capable of hiding several. In contrast Berneray has eight possible chamber tombs of which all but one are located at intervals along the top of the back slope to the northern seashore. None of these examples have any distinctive passage structure and many are only several unusually large stone slabs apparently set within a cairn of mounded earth and stone. If these are indeed Neolithic rather than Bronze Age burial chambers then their spaced location, quite suggestive of single family tombs being used as land holding markers, is unusual.

The use of such burial monuments as territorial markers is possible, but in the Borve valley the two tombs appear to act more like medieval parish churches acting as a focus for the community rather than marking the boundary of its holdings. Although Dun Bharpa is not right on the crest of the northern side of the valley it is located in a skyline position relative to any settlement in the valley below.

The comparison that has often been made in this chapter between our islands of the southern Outer Hebrides and the Northern Isles is no accident. It is a reflection in many ways of the influences that appear to have flowed from the north to the west. Orkney is thought to be one of the major core areas in the British Isles for much of the early Neolithic, only later being eclipsed by the powerful society that emerged in the region of Wessex culminating in the transformation of the Marlborough Downs into a ritual landscape of European importance.

Apart from the resonating influence of the Orcadian ritual architecture, the distinctive Grooved Ware and Unstan style of pottery also appears to emanate outwards from the Northern Isles. This perception of the northern periphery being a broadcaster of change rather than a receptor fits well the concept of indigenous populations absorbing the new ways of thought and action, impressing their own identity upon the system and bouncing it back with the fundamentalist power of the newly converted. The Outer Hebrides may be considered as being part of this process in a similar manner to that of the Northern Isles with the possible formation of an embryonic core area beginning to emerge as some of its ritual architectural peculiarities indicate. In size and complexity the monuments at Callanish are impressive by any European standard and in ceramics the 'Hebridean Ware' style pottery is a distinctive local development. However, the impulse does not appear strong enough to withstand the power of Orcadian influences and it is overshadowed by them.

The Western Isles were also subject to a fundamental disadvantage – the geographical marginality of the islands at the north-western edge of Europe – from which stemmed a range of disabling factors that include the inclement climate, the short growing season, and the formation of blanket bog and acid peat soil. There is also the unfortunate lack of resources in general and especially timber due to the depletion of the woodland. The almost total absence of workable flint, that mainstay of the new Stone Age, may have been particularly crippling.

When we published our early interim reports on the excavations at Alt Chrisal our excitement translated the site into something of greater importance than was probably justifiable, but in the light of our work in the southern islands we find that we are still excited by the archaeological remains. No, we did not expect another Skara Brae; but as the great cairn of Dun Bharpa clearly shows, the ability, social strength and demographic factors were all in place and we do think that a Hebridean equivalent – not so grand since the geology will not allow it – may be there waiting to be found.

3 Ritual landscapes

By the end of the third millennium BC, the landscape of our islands would have
looked somewhat different to how it appeared to the first settlers 2000 years earlier.
The steady decline in tree cover had by now removed most of the birch and hazel,
but small numbers of pine, alder and oak were still to be seen, especially in the
more sheltered locations. With the disappearance of the trees had come the
expansion of waterlogged soils, the spread of heathland and rough grazing, and the
development of blanket peat over some of the higher and bleaker areas. Human
settlements were still few in number and concentrated around the coasts, but the
sheep pastures spread inland and played their part in clearing the landscape of trees.
Scattered through the landscape were the megalithic chambered tombs – a handful
beneath prominent stone cairns, but many, especially on the smaller islands,
beneath small mounds of earth and stone. Some of them had by now been in the
landscape for perhaps a millennium and, though they were probably regarded as
venerated sites and may have played an important role in claims to territory and
identity, they were probably by now embedded and passive spectators rather than
active participants in the life of the islands.

That role was now being taken on by new types of monument which were not
funerary sites at all, although they may have been linked with concepts of ancestry
and ancestors in the minds of those who built them. Indeed, the great neolithic
passage grave at Dun Bharpa incorporated the essential features of these monuments
many centuries before the first of them were erected. Its ring of upright monoliths
anticipates both the individual standing stone and the stone circle. At the opposite
end of the island chain, the stone circle and upright monoliths at Callanish may have
been erected as early as 3000 BC, so it is possible that the standing stones and stone
circles on our islands date to the earlier rather than the later third millennium BC.
Equally, the use of upright stones as markers in the landscape has continued in the
islands into recent times and we cannot always be sure that one of our 'standing
stones' was first erected in prehistory. And, needless to say, some of 'the standing
stones' no longer stand, but lie, in the landscape.

Barra and its neighbouring islands are not blessed with an abundance of
naturally long, relatively slim, slabs of stone, and we have to bear this in mind when
looking at potential standing stones (and indeed stone circles). We believe we can
recognise 12-15 ancient standing stones in the southern isles. Seven of them are
found on Barra, and these are the most convincing and impressive examples. The
best-known are the pair of stones, 3.2m and 2.8m long, on a small shelf of land
overlooking Brevig bay on the east coast (**colour plate 17**). They are matched by

a second pair, originally at least 2.9m and 1.7m long, on the machair on Borve headland on the west coast. From this pair one can look westwards up the Borve valley to the Pass-of-the-Mouth – a natural routeway from west to east across the island. Almost on the watershed of the Pass lies the largest of the stones, nearly 6m long with almost straight sides and a tapered end which appears to have been artificially shaped by breaking flakes of stone off the edges. This stone would have dominated the view right down the valley and out to the headland. On the northern watershed of the same valley is another stone, 3m long, and lying only 100m from Dun Bharpa with its ring of stones. A seventh stone on Barra is found overlooking the Gortein valley and its small bay on the south coast of the island. It is a regularly shaped monolith 2.4m long, around which are traces of a wall or stone setting. It is hard to believe it was not once set upright.

Vatersay provides three examples, varying in size from 1.7m to 2.2m, only one of which still stands. The largest of the three lies adjacent to a gap in a major land boundary which divides the eastern arm of south Vatersay in two. To the south of Vatersay, three possible examples are found on Sandray, two overlooking bays at the north and south ends of the island respectively, and a third perched on a cliff-face looking into the Minches. But all are under 2m tall, and the smallest stands only 0.6m above ground. The only possible example on Mingulay is equally stunted (0.8m above ground), but its position close to a megalithic chamber and overlooking Mingulay Bay foster our suspicions that it is a significant monument. Finally, on the southernmost island of Berneray the only convincing example to be seen, a regular monolith 1.2m tall, must be dubious because it stands right alongside the trackway constructed in early modern times.

There has been much debate, over many years, as to the meaning and purpose of standing stones. Where they are found in alignments and/or associated with stone circles then their involvement in ritual of some kind seems likely. It has been suggested recently that stones, whether in circles, alignments or standing alone, may be associated with ancestors/the dead, whereas timber circles and alignments may be concerned with rituals of life and the living. At Dun Bharpa there is clearly an association between the dead, buried in the tomb chamber, and the ring of upright stones set around the edge of the cairn which covers them. We shall see later in this chapter that an association between standing stones and the dead may have persisted into the late second millennium BC on Barra. But whether we can extrapolate from these relatively rare examples and ascribe similar associations to stones standing in isolation is obviously debatable. Standing stones on their own, or even in pairs, are more open to other interpretations. Looking at the standing stones we have identified on the islands two impressions emerge. The first is that the majority of them are distinctly unimpressive – of 15 possible examples only two are more than 3m in height. The majority therefore were probably not intended to be either dominant or prominent in the landscape. The second impression concerns their location. Nine of the stones immediately overlook bays, in each case with a small, reasonably fertile valley behind it. Three more stand on boundaries – natural watersheds or in one case a man-made linear bank. All these stones might be regarded as territorial markers of some sort, and the concept that the stones in someway embodied 'the ancestors' would not be alien to this interpretation. Whether they were ever the focus of ritual or ceremony, except perhaps at the time of their erection, is arguable.

Stone circles on the other hand are interpreted by most prehistorians as foci for repeated communal ritual action, though how frequently and for what purpose is open to speculation. But we have to say at once that there is not a single monument on any of the islands that we would dignify with the designation 'stone circle'. Such a term conjures up visions of tall stones, set in large, nearly circular arrangements. Nothing like this is to be seen on Barra and its neighbours, and we prefer to call them 'stone rings'. The monuments are small in size, constructed with mostly very modest boulders, and are rarely even approximately circular. Fortunately they are not alone. In Argyll and some of the islands of the Inner Hebrides stone circles are mostly between 5m and 20m in diameter, clearly oval rather than circular, and with few stones as much as a metre tall. Aubrey Burl has noted that such features are characteristic of most, though certainly not all, the stone 'circles' in the Western Isles. Furthermore, excavations at Machrie Moor on Arran revealed that two such stone rings there post-dated Beaker land-use, and therefore were probably constructed in the early second millennium BC. The C14 evidence obtained from other stone circles and rings in north and west Britain supports the view that many were not built until after 2000 BC.

As long ago as 1794 the Reverend Edward MacQueen said of Barra 'here also are several Druidical temples, none of them remarkable for extent or structure', and in an eighteenth-century context it is difficult to believe he referred to anything other than stone rings or circles. But none have ever been recorded by the Royal Commission, the Ordnance Survey, Prof. Alexander Thom or Dr Aubrey Burl. It was therefore with some surprise but also some trepidation that in our very first season of work on Barra we recorded a site as a stone ring. The site, which we labelled B55, stood on a knoll projecting into the centre of the Borve valley. To the north the cairn of Dun Bharpa is clearly visible on the skyline, and the chambered cairn at Balnacraig is also visible to the north-west. The stone setting had clearly been disturbed and modified on one or more occasions, but it still gave the distinct impression of having originally been a roughly circular arrangement of about a dozen stones. In 1992 we made a detailed plan of the site, and in 1995 we excavated a segment of it, hoping to discover more about its original form, and also of course some cultural material that might point to its period of use. The 'circle' proved to be an oval about 17 x 13m, demarcated by an alignment of 10 large blocks of stone, the tallest of which was 1.2m high. Our excavation area included one of the 'gaps' in the ring, as well as some of the standing stones, and we found that the standing stones were surrounded by a halo of smaller stones which probably came from small packing mounds around the base of the upright stones. In the 'gap' we found similar halos with an empty space at the centre, confirming our suspicion that two stones had been removed from the ring at some point in time. We were disappointed, but not in the least surprised, that no cultural material at all was found in the excavated area. Nevertheless, the excavation confirmed that there had originally been a ring of at least 12 stones, and these stones were not simply rolled or dumped in place, but that some care had been taken to embed each stone in a small mound of cobbles around its base. On the north side of the monument, a U-shaped stone setting about 3.5m long forms what might elsewhere be labelled a 'cove', but whether this is part of the original design or was erected at a much later date we cannot say.

Survey subsequently revealed six further potential stone rings on Barra, one on Vatersay and two on Mingulay (**colour plate 15**). Six of these, including those on Vatersay and Mingulay, were very small: 4-7m in diameter, with between eight and twelve stones, the largest of them only 0.7-1.1m in height. There seemed little similarity in their locations. The two on Mingulay were on small shelves on steep slopes above cliffs, while those on Vatersay and above Glen on Barra were at the base of slopes below high hills. Another at Brevig is on a small platform near the floor of the valley, and a second is several hundred metres upslope in rough pasture.

Of the remaining three rings, all on Barra, that on a flat-topped hill overlooking the natural harbour of Northbay is the most impressive. It is more or less circular, about 23m in diameter, with 10 stones apparently in situ, and perhaps two to four removed. The biggest stone here is 1.3m in length. Another ring at Brevig is notable for being very oval, 21 x 10m, with eleven stones remaining but possibly as many again missing.

Finally, yet another ring at Brevig is the most interesting in terms of its later treatment. It has been so modified and robbed that its original size and design are not easily established. As it survives it appears to have been a ring about 16 x 14m, but some of the stones on one side have been moved and the arc straightened (**17**). We suspect that originally the ring was circular, about 14m in diameter. Fifteen stones remain more in less situ, but as many more may have made up the complete ring. The tallest stones are on the east side, where the biggest stands 1.5m high. The missing stones are to be found in a series of small clearance cairns immediately to one side of the ring. Each of these cairns is focused around one large stone between 0.8m and 1m long. These cairns clearly point to a decision at some point in time, and probably in the post-medieval era, to clear this low hillock for cultivation. But not only were half the stones left in place, but the hillock was never in fact properly cultivated. When the sun is low one can see that the entire area around the stone ring has been lazy-bedded, probably for potatoes, but that the hillock on which the ring stands, and on which these clearance cairns are situated, has no lazy-beds. The impression is that after the decision to clear the ring had been taken, the people had second thoughts about its removal and decided to leave the ground uncultivated.

This may say something about how the eighteenth- or nineteenth-century inhabitants viewed these rings, but it does not of course provide any insights into why they were constructed in the first place. Stone rings have always been regarded as the sites of prehistoric ritual, and over the past 50 years controversy has raged over the extent to which they could have been used as lunar or solar observatories. Our rings are too

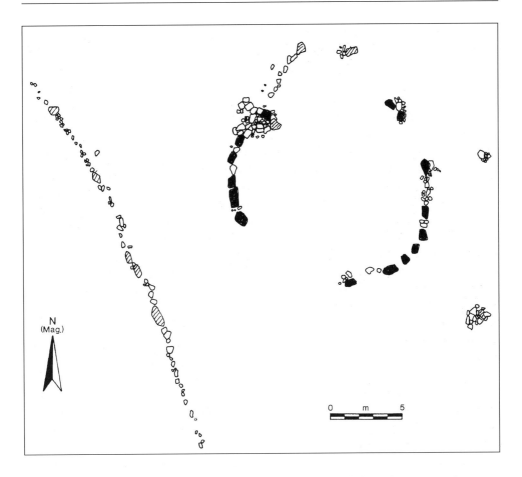

17 A modified stone ring at Brevig, Barra. Originally a ring of about 30 stones, 15 are more or less in situ (black) but half (hatched) have been removed and used in nearby modern boundaries or put on clearance cairns

disturbed, and also too insignificant in terms of their location and the size of their stones, to be convincingly interpreted as observatories. But this is not to deny the possibility, even probability, that they were used for ceremonies in which the sun and/or the moon played a role. It is still however difficult to understand why they were located where they were.

We have already noted the diversity of their locations, some apparently looking seawards, others in low-lying areas at the edge of valleys, and only those at Northbay and Borve in a position that one might call either dominant or conspicuous.

At least on Barra we might speculate that the rings were located to serve four natural zones: Northbay, the north of the island, Borve the west, Glen the south, and Brevig the east. But Brevig may have been something more than a local centre for ritual. It is here on the southern side of one small valley overlooking Brevig bay that we have four possible stone rings, as well as two impressive standing stones.

18 An elongated cist, T180, as discovered above Bretadale, at 200m OD, covered with heather and partly buried under peat

This is a remarkable concentration of apparently ritual monuments and raises the possibility that Brevig was a ceremonial centre for the whole island in the early second millennium BC.

A second island-wide focus, albeit for rituals of a very different sort, may have been situated on the opposite side of the island on a high ridge overlooking the prettily named but remote and rather bleak Bretadale. When one of the survey teams came back and reported they had found four or five megalithic tombs clustered above Bretadale we were excited, intrigued, but also somewhat sceptical, particularly as they insisted there was no trace of covering cairns. So we went to have a look for ourselves. What we found were roughly oblong settings of stones, ranging in length from about 6m to 9m, between 1.5m and 2.5m wide (**18**). The largest stones in each structure were a metre or more in height, but many stones were smaller. We noticed the largest stones were always at one end, which was the end 'closed' by a continuous line of uprights. The other end was either open, or had only a few small blocks across it. We also noted that the 'closed' end was usually wider than the other end, so the settings were slightly wedge-shaped. Careful searching through the heather eventually revealed eight of these structures, all located on this single ridge overlooking Bretadale. They were so embedded that we felt they must be ancient rather than modern, and they

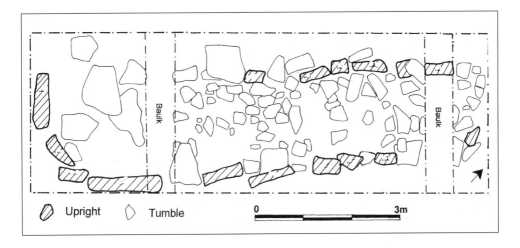

Upright   Tumble   0   3m

19 Plan of the elongated cist T180 as revealed by excavation. The tallest upright stones (hatched) are at the closed, west end of the monument. Two C14 dates suggest the enclosure was going out of use soon after 2000 BC

certainly had a megalithic look about them. But what were they? We decided to excavate one of them.

T180 proved to be 9.2m long, oriented with its closed end to the west (**19**). Its west end was 2.8m wide, and its east end, with a line of small blocks across it, was 2.2m. The biggest stone used in the structure, a block 1 x 1.2m, stood bang in the middle of the west end. All the stones in the south wall were 0.8-1m high, but there were fewer big stones in the north wall, the gaps between them being filled with smaller blocks which had apparently been placed one on another to make up the height. Inside fallen monoliths and a scatter of smaller blocks were embedded at different levels in the peat infill, suggesting the structure had collapsed slowly over a long period of time. The peat infill was about 2ft (60cm) deep, and when it was all removed bedrock lay immediately underneath. We had not expected to find any bones in this soil, even if they had been there in the first place, but we had hoped for perhaps some pottery or flints that might help us date the structure. But there was nothing at all! All was not lost however. We noted that not only was there no buried soil or land-surface under the peat infill, but that the stones of the wall were placed directly on bedrock. In other words, when the structure was built the bedrock had been cleared of whatever soil lay on it, and the structure had been built not only directly on bedrock, but with a totally clear rock surface inside it. We therefore took samples from the base of the peat infill in two places for carbon dating. When the dates came through from the lab they gave brackets for the beginning of the peat infill of some time between about 1950 and 1450 BC. This would be the time by which the structures had been abandoned. So our suspicions that they were prehistoric monuments were confirmed. But we still had to try to work out what they had been used for.

We had essentially four pieces of evidence which, taken together, might point to an answer. First there was the shape and construction of the monuments. Their slightly wedge-shaped and megalithic appearance could be compared to the chambers of some of the Scottish chamber tombs. But the similarities were very general, and two key differences were that whereas the tomb chambers were roofed and then covered by cairns, ours revealed no trace of either feature. On the other hand, the collection of large megalithic slabs which were then carefully used to build a tall wall or facade at one end, suggests more than a casual or random use of building material. The second piece of evidence is the way in which the structures were apparently kept clean throughout their period of use. Whilst the absence of bones can be explained by the nature of the soil, that of pottery and flint cannot. If the structures were used for living in, even on a seasonal basis, one might expect some material debris to be left within them. Equally, burials in megalithic structures were usually accompanied by small quantities of grave-goods, even in the Outer Hebrides. Thirdly we considered the location of these structures. They are very exposed in terms of both weather and visibility. For this reason they would not be suitable either as homes or as hideaways in times of hostility. Equally, the high, exposed position of the structures makes it unlikely they would have been used as store-places or sheep pens. Finally we have to take into account the uniqueness of these monuments. The eight examples found on this single ridge above Bretadale are the only ones known anywhere in our islands. This alone suggests that they were something 'special' – a type of monument used for a particular purpose which was not replicated elsewhere. The only explanation we could find which might fit all the pieces of evidence was that they were mortuary enclosures, where the dead were exposed until defleshing was complete, at which point the bones would be collected and removed for burial or disposal elsewhere. Such enclosures were built and used in other parts of Britain in the third millennium BC, so these structures could be part of a broad tradition of funerary practice.

If our interpretation is right, we are still left with two important and unanswered questions. The first is whether the enclosures were all in use at once, or were built and used one after another. The answer to that question will not only affect the period of time over which the monuments were in use but also the likely size of the group which used each enclosure. If they succeeded one another, then the builders and users could have been successive generations of a single family or group. If they were all in use together it is more likely they represent several groups – at least eight perhaps!

There is of course no direct evidence to answer this question, but because we have no similar monuments anywhere else on Barra we believe it more likely that the structures were all in use at the same time and they were built and used by several groups. If the groups were essentially kin-groups, perhaps extended families, then seven or eight groups each of 10-20 people might well represent the entire population of the island at this time.

20 Kerbed cairn VS4B, on Huilish headland, Vatersay, after the removal of turf. Note the neat level-topped kerb, and the small stones used as the final covering of the cairn

The remaining question is what happened to the defleshed bones that were collected from the enclosures? There are four possibilities. One is that they were simply disposed of – perhaps thrown into the sea or scattered across the landscape. Another is that they were collected up and buried within one of the great chamber tombs like Dun Bharpa. Excavated chamber tombs elsewhere in the Hebrides have yielded pieces of Beaker pottery as well as earlier material, so the tombs were perhaps still in use at the time when these enclosures were built. But this would be stretching the chronology a little, and there do not seem to be enough chamber tombs to go round. Another possibility is that the bones were taken away and buried in small cists. We found five such cists on Barra, all about 2km south-east of Bretadale. The one excavated example yielded no dating or burial evidence at all, although a sixth cist found built onto the back of roundhouse T19 yielded an almost complete Beaker but no bone material. Rectangular burial cists are commonly associated with Beaker pottery in Britain, so the cists and the Bretadale enclosures may well have been contemporaries. But the small number of cists we found, and their very limited distribution, does not fit well with the hypothesis that the enclosures were used by extended kin-groups from all over the island for several generations.

The fourth possibility is that the bones were removed for burial beneath a cairn. In terms of numbers alone this is a more likely scenario – we have 14 identified burial cairns on Barra, and they are found in various parts of the island rather than clustered

21 Cremation pyre material at the centre of cairn VS4B. It contains small pieces of burnt bone, but the amount of debris is too small to have come from a funerary pyre on the spot

in a single small area. But were they contemporary with the supposed mortuary enclosures, and do the human remains buried beneath them support the notion that they may have been collected from elsewhere for final burial?

Answers to these questions can only come from excavated cairns, and fortunately we worked on two cairns on Vatersay which go some way to answering these questions. The Vatersay cairns were located at about 120m above sea level, on the neck of Huilish Point (**colour plate 7**), overlooking the beautiful beach of West Bay from the south. They were about 250m apart, separated from each other by a small valley, but clearly intervisible. The larger cairn was over 8m in diameter and surrounded by a ring of stone blocks, carefully laid so that their upper surfaces formed a more or less level kerb around the entire cairn. The cairn stood 0.8m high and had probably never stood much higher. The smaller cairn, with a similar neatly laid kerb, was a little under 8m in diameter and also stood about 0.8m high (**20**). As we excavated these cairns we became increasingly aware that there was much more to their construction that simply dumping a mound of stones over a burial area and enclosing the cairn in a kerb.

The smaller cairn proved to be a particularly complex structure. It had been built directly on a fine, sandy, mostly stone-free soil that appeared to have been cultivated. The large quantity of smallish field stones incorporated into the cairn material supports this impression. An oval arrangement of small stone blocks was laid on this soil, and just to one side of it six oblong blocks were laid in an arc which followed

22 The inner cairn construction within cairn VS4B, edged with a rough temporary kerb before being engulfed in the larger final cairn

the line of the oval. Within the oval, some slabs were laid flat and a group of cobbles were laid on these slabs together with a large much-worn stone 'rubber'. On the cobbles was a deposit of bright orange-brown clayey soil, flecked with red and black, containing many tiny fragments of white bone (**21**). It was immediately recognisable as debris from a pyre, so it appears that the cairn was covering a cremation. But this 'pyre' deposit was small and thin, and lacking any ash, and most of the stones outlining the oval were completely unburnt.

We suspected therefore that this was not the funerary pyre itself, but a selected sample of it, brought from elsewhere for burial beneath the cairn. That is, the cairn was not the site of the cremation. This was confirmed by measuring the magnetism of the pyre material and the stone cobbles immediately beneath it. Whilst the pyre debris revealed very high magnetism, the stones immediately under it were very low. The pyre cannot have been fired over the stones. Where the cremation actually took place is unknown, although in both cairns we found white beach pebbles incorporated into the deposits over the pyre debris and so perhaps the cremations had taken place on the beach below. The pyre debris was overlain by flat slabs, in turn covered with a thin layer of apparently cultivated soil. It was over this soil that burnt cobbles and beach pebbles were deposited (**colour plate 18**). There was now a low oval cairn on the site, and this was covered with a thick layer of pure black soil, perhaps from a midden or occupation site, but well sorted as it contained

23 A metre-long standing stone buried in cairn VS4B. The stone immediately stood out as quite different to any other stone in the monument by reason of its regularity and length. Its end is buried under the kerb of the inner cairn, at left

only two flint flakes. The earth mound was then encased in a stone cairn, formed by placing large blocks in a ring and using smaller stones to cover the earth mound with a stone dome (**22**). During the building of this inner stone cairn, a narrow flat slab of stone over a metre long was laid against the cairn at an angle of about 35° (**23**). There was no other stone remotely like it in the cairn; it was a better example of a standing stone than some of those we found and recorded elsewhere. We have already noted earlier the association of the ring of standing stones with the great cairn at Dun Bharpa and suggested that there is a connection between standing stones, funerary monuments and ancestors. This example, found buried in a kerbed cairn, reiterates that connection, and is in fact supported by four other examples of apparently fallen standing stones associated with cairns. One example, about 1.2m long, was found on a 4m diameter cairn on Mingulay, and another

1 *Berneray and Barra Head lighthouse from Mingulay; note the vertical cliffs and grass-covered north-facing aspect*

2 *Dun Briste, Berneray, looking towards Mingulay. The pink sea-thrift indicates that spray from the sea 180m below blows across this bleak headland*

3 *Dun Mingulay, fronted by a slowly eroding dyke with vertically embedded rocks*

4   *Mingulay Bay, seen from the south, with Pabbay in the distance. Note the smooth contours and absence of trees*

5   *The ruins of Mingulay village, being engulfed by the dunes, with the priests house upslope to the rear (1991)*

6 *The defensive location of Dun Sandray, perched on a rocky knoll, overlooking Loch na Cuilce*

7 *West Bay, Vatersay, overlooked by Dun Vatersay on the green hill to the south; a cemetery of four kerbed cairns lies on the slope west of the Dun*

8 *The Borve valley with its pastures and, in the distance, the machair on Borve headland, west Barra*

9 *Traigh Eias (west beach) and the Eoligarry machair from Ben Erival, with Dun Scurriavl on the headland in the distance, north Barra*

10 An early Neolithic stone-lined hearth of about 3000 BC on the working platform at Alt Chrisal, Barra

11 The beaker found in a cist at roundhouse T19, Alt Chrisal, with zones of incised and cord-impressed decoration

12 The roundhouse T19 at the moment of discovery 1989; on excavation it proved to date to the late third millennium BC

13 *The paved or flat cairn, T214, overlooking the Sound of Vatersay, after excavation (and a rainstorm!)*

14 *The great cairn covering the passage grave of Dun Bharpa, with its ring of monoliths set in the perimeter*

15 An unimpressive stone ring (MY49) on the south coast of Mingulay

16 A much-denuded kerbed cairn on Fuday, with a small standing stone set within it

17 *The remaining upright standing stone at Brevig, Barra; a second stone, now in pieces, lies close by*

18 *The cremation platform under kerbed cairn VS4B, Vatersay; the small cobbles lie immediately on a small mound of pyre material*

19 *The Bronze Age (?) cellular house in the dunes on Pabbay; this may be one of several similar structures in these dunes*

20 The upright stone 'facade' in chamber A of the Pabbay cellular house

21 Section of a roundhouse MY384, built in the dunes in Mingulay Bay. Note the depth of the deposits within, and the large wall stones to the right of the excavator

22 A well-preserved wheelhouse at an altitude of around 600ft (180m) above sea level on Cadha Mor, Barra

23 The surviving arc of walling at the Pabbay broch; note the 'window' in the centre of the arc, and the remains of a second near the camera

24 The remains of Dun Clieff on a tidal islet, on the west coast of Barra; it is difficult to imagine a more exposed location

25 The broch and causeway at Bagh Hirivagh, Barra; the building of the causeway may have required as much stone as the construction of the broch

26 The Pabbay Pictish symbol stone, just under a metre long

27 The stone-clad early burial mound on Pabbay, with the symbol stone lying at the foot of the slope

28 Medieval shielings at Allasdale, Barra, overlying substantial round houses of probably Iron Age date

29 *The early Christian churchyard at Kilbarr; the north chapel to the right has been restored, but St Kilbarr's church, to the left, has lost its gable ends*

30 *Relict lazybeds, overlain by a sheep wall of probably mid-nineteenth-century date, at Caolis, Vatersay*

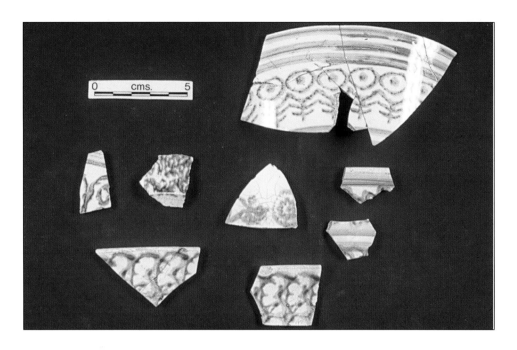

31 Scottish spongeware from a blackhouse at Balnabodach; this 'cheap and cheerful' table-ware was popular at Balnabodach

32 The sea-wall of Macneil's chemical factory, North Bay; note the blocked portals, with their thresholds at high water mark, through which made-kelp and peat could be delivered to the factory by boat

33 The cleared settlement of Balnabodach on the shore of Loch Obe, Barra. The houses cleared in 1851 are on this side of the stream; some of the standing buildings beyond were occupied into the twentieth century

34 Reconstructed log cabin, c.1800, Highland Village, Cape Breton, the type of house that most early Barra emigrants first occupied

15

35 The landscape of Vernon River, Prince Edward Island; Roderick Macneil of Brevig settled amongst the trees on the right in 1803

36 The Macdonald House, built 1829, Highland Village, Cape Breton. Immigrant Hebridean families were already building two-storied houses with several separate rooms within a decade or two or emigration

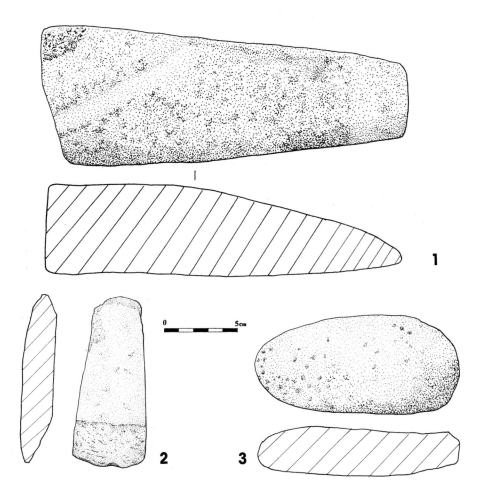

24 Stone ard and axe rough-outs, and a stone rubber, cairn VS4B. The rubber was found beneath the pyre material, the axe rough-out near the top of the final cairn, and the ard rough-out on a kerbstone; all appeared to have been quite deliberately placed

(apparently still upright and buried within the cairn) was noted in a cairn on the offshore island of Fuday (**colour plate 16**). On Barra, cairns above Alt Chrisal and Greian had fallen stones almost 1m long at their periphery.

The standing stone and the inner cairn that it was laid against were now surrounded by the kerbstones, and the gap between kerb and inner cairn was filled with a spread of medium sized stone blocks. Finally, the whole monument was covered with small field-stones, so that on completion the cairn had a profile like an upturned soup-bowl. Using small field-stones to complete the cairn may simply have been a labour-saving device – the stones were on hand and putting them on the cairn helped to further clear the cultivated land around it. But we believe it may have had a deeper significance than this. We have already noted the deposition of a stone 'rubber', probably used with a saddle quern to grind grain, beneath the pyre debris, and the layer of cultivated soil incorporated into the inner cairn. On the kerb of the cairn we also found a rough-out of a stone ard (plough) tip, and almost at the centre point of the cairn an imitation axe made from gneiss (**24**). There seems to be a repeated statement about arable land in the history of the cairn's construction, and we wonder therefore whether the completion of the cairn with field-stones was part of this same story. Did the entire community attend the burial at the cairn, and did they each toss on a handful of field-stones in the same way that modern mourners may still toss a handful of earth onto a coffin?

Although we found no grave goods with the cremation, both our excavated cairns produced a small quantity of artefacts, some of which help to date the construction of the cairns. In addition to the rubber, ard tip and imitation axe, the cairn incorporated a handful of pieces of flint including two end scrapers and an awl. About 20 sherds of pottery were found in the larger cairn, and 15 in a deposit under the smaller one. The pottery from the two cairns was in different fabrics, and that from the smaller cairn may have come from a single thick-walled storage jar we thought might be of Middle or late Bronze Age date. We sent sherds from the two cairns to colleagues at Durham for dating by 'Optically Stimulated Luminescence', and although the error brackets were wider than we hoped, the results were very interesting. The larger cairn incorporated sherds which were made sometime between 2500 and 1500 BC, and the smaller overlay sherds dated to 1450-650 BC. They were thus almost certainly separated in time by at least some centuries. The date of the smaller cairn was also suggested by fragments of a bronze cloak-fastener found in the body of the cairn material. This probably dates to the later Bronze Age.

The earlier of the cairns, therefore, would have probably been more or less contemporary with our stone enclosures on Bretadale. Given that the cairns did not cover complete burials but only the remains of cremated bones, they could have been the final resting place for bones which were first defleshed in the Bretadale enclosures, before subsequent cremation and burial. On islands where wood for fuel was in very short supply, we might glimpse the rationale behind the development of a two-stage process which greatly reduced the amount of fuel needed for cremation by reducing the body first to bones. But if fuel for cremations was a problem, why was cremation adopted as a preferred method of finally disposing of the dead? We can only suppose that the beliefs and symbolism behind cremation were powerful factors in the development of funerary behaviour.

One could go even further and speculate that, since the megalithic enclosures are found only in the one location on Barra, but burial cairns are found on all the islands south of Barra as well as on Barra itself, Bretadale served as the preliminary mortuary site for the whole island group. But fascinating as that suggestion is, on balance we think this is unlikely. One reason for rejecting the idea is that, in constructing their burial cairns, the communities on the islands south of Barra show a degree of variation from the norm on Barra, which might be interpreted as expressions of their own identities within the overall cairn tradition.

The 14 cairns we recorded on Barra are mostly of a type we called a 'bordered' cairn. These have a ring of stones around their perimeter, but the stones are not laid to form a level kerb, instead including many blocks set upright, forming a serrated border to the cairn. Inside this border, the mound of stones rises immediately to form a low bowl-shaped cairn. Smaller numbers of 'kerbed' cairns, like the two we excavated on Vatersay, are found on Barra, although two are found on each of the offshore islands to the north and west, Fuday and Fuiay (**colour plate 16**). In contrast, the kerbed cairns are a very popular monument on Vatersay. There are almost 30 known examples, in addition to seven bordered cairns. Bearing in mind that Vatersay is only a sixth the size of Barra, you could say that it has 30 times as many kerbed cairns! For its size, Sandray too is well-populated with cairns, but none of its 10 appear to be kerbed, and all but one are small – between 2m and 4m in diameter. Pabbay presents a similar picture. Mingulay reveals a comparable density but only three of its 20-plus cairns are kerbed. On the other hand the majority are over 4m in diameter. In contrast Berneray has no convincing examples at all. The differences between the islands in terms of their burial cairns is summarised in the table below:

	Kerbed	Bordered	Av. diam.	Density*
Barra	6	8	5.1m	1:1050
Vatersay	29	7	6.2m	1:67
Sandray	0	10	3.4m	1:97
Pabbay	0	7	3.9m	1:90
Mingulay	3	19	4.7m	1:72
Berneray	0	0	–	–

(* expressed as 1 cairn to X acres of land)

Barra thus seems to be something of a poor relation in terms of the number of Bronze Age cairns it contains relative to its size, and we might speculate that the Bretadale enclosures represent one element of an alternative funerary process to that found on its satellite islands.

We suggested the Bretadale enclosures might each have been used by a different family group, over a period of several or even many generations. The cairns, on the evidence of the two excavated examples, cannot be seen in the same way. There was only a single burial episode, and although the few tiny cremated bone fragments allow of no certainty, it is likely that each cairn represents the burial of a single individual. In the case of the larger of the excavated cairns, the skeletal evidence pointed to an adult male. Group or family affiliations are however sometimes suggested by the appearance of cairns, usually kerbed cairns, in pairs or even in cemeteries. Pairs of cairns are found on Fuday, Fuiay, at Borve and above Crubisdale on Barra, on Ben Rulibreck and south of Dun Vatersay, and on the north slope of McPhee's Hill and the top of Carnan on Mingulay. The larger of our excavated Vatersay cairns was one of a pair, and the smaller was in a close-set line of four. But the most remarkable group was found in the small valley west of

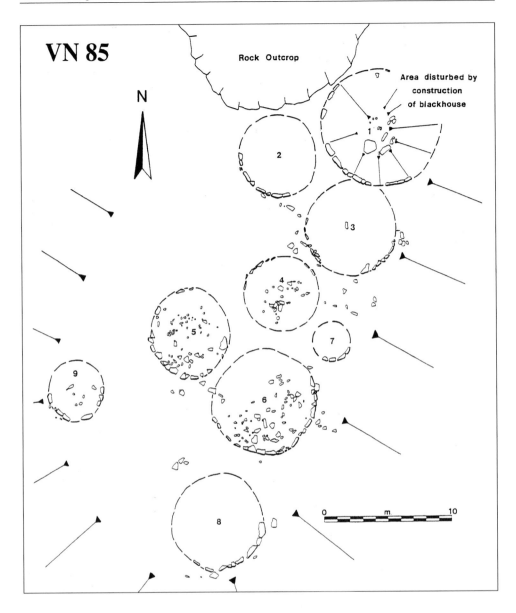

VN 85

Rock Outcrop

Area disturbed by
construction
of blackhouse

N

25 The cemetery of nine kerbed cairns at Tresivick, Vatersay. Nine other cairns are nearby, all on the east side of the stream which runs down this small valley

Tresivick looking south into West Bay on Vatersay. We called it 'Death Valley' because we found 18 kerbed cairns in an area only 250m square. Even within this confined space, they formed four separate clusters of two, three, four and nine cairns. The largest group were crammed onto a little knoll that rose above the floor of the valley, and ranged from a 9m diameter monster to a neat little cairn less than 3m across (**25**). This must surely be some sort of family necropolis, but if each cairn

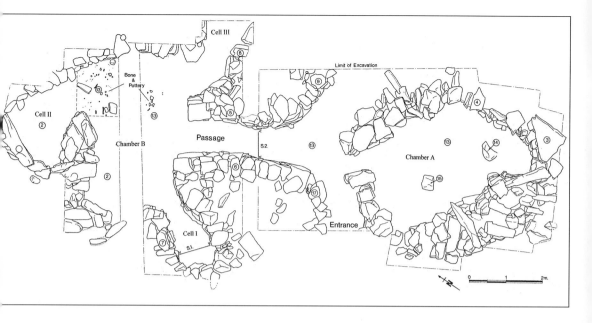

26 The plan of the Bronze Age (?) 'cellular' house on Pabbay, a subterranean structure dug into the sand

contains the bones of just one individual, do they represent an entire family or just selected individuals from a succession of generations? And what was the relationship between the people buried on this hillock and those buried in the three smaller clusters nearby?

If we knew about the settlements of the living at this time it might help us to approach these questions, but identifying Bronze Age settlement sites from surface remains with little or no disturbance of the buried deposits is almost impossible. In 'Death Valley' we were tempted to identify four or five roundhouse sites on the west side of the valley, across a stream from the cemetery area, as the contemporary settlement, but on the basis of evidence from excavated houses elsewhere they appeared (from surface indications) to be too large for Bronze Age homes and more likely to be Iron Age. We have seen in the previous chapter that at the time when Beaker style pottery was in use, and stone circles or rings were being erected, people living at Alt Chrisal were occupying a circular stone-and-earth walled hut about 4.5m diameter. A similar but slightly larger hut in the Borve valley, dating to the earlier first millennium BC, is described below. We think it likely therefore that such huts were in use throughout the so-called Bronze Age, but without excavation we cannot confidently ascribe individual examples known only from field survey to this period. In half a dozen cases however the nearby presence of one or more Bronze Age burial cairns perhaps strengthens the possibility that the huts belong to this era.

New types of houses may have emerged during the second millennium BC, however, particularly in areas on the machair where they could be dug into the sand.

In South Uist our colleague Mike Parker Pearson had already found both figure-of-eight (or double) roundhouses, and multi-cellular houses dating to the end of the Late Bronze Age. Stone blocks and slabs found in the dunes on Pabbay attracted our attention and a sampling excavation revealed a subterranean multi-cellular structure here too (**colour plate 19**). A narrow passage linked two sub-circular chambers, in one of which there were three small cells built into the wall (**26**). Some of the architecture was quite impressive, with slabs of gneiss set upright to form a facade (**colour plate 20**). These uprights may have supported the roof structure and lintel stones, some of which were found collapsed into one of the chambers. The floor of the structure yielded about three dozen pieces of pottery and a similar number of animal bones. The pottery is probably middle or late Bronze Age, and the animals bones are all from sheep except for a fragment of cattle horncore. Surface indications suggest one or two similar structures nearby, so we may have a small community rather than an isolated family farmstead. If such houses are found on South Uist and Pabbay, then we must assume that they probably also existed on Barra, Vatersay and Sandray, but are still buried beneath the machair or the dunes.

Elsewhere around the coast of Barra another type of temporary occupation site appears. These are oval or circular areas enclosed by a rough ring or bank of stones. Although the activities which went on in these areas are not easily identified from the surviving evidence, later in the Bronze Age they may have become a regular feature of the coastal landscape. Less than 2km west of Alt Chrisal we excavated inside an oval area marked out by a ring of boulders. It had a turf-built windbreak erected inside it, and a fireplace, and produced a large quantity of knapping debris from flint-working. Although there was no pottery at all, we managed to get a C14 date which placed the use of the enclosure around 800-600 BC, at the end of the Bronze Age. Subsequently we have encountered two rather similar structures, one on the north coast of the island, and one on the east, both of which have yielded lithic material but no pottery. Unexcavated examples have been found on the west coast of Barra, on Vatersay and perhaps on Sandray. Situated as they all are right on the edge of the sea, we believe that the activities centred there must have been concerned with exploiting marine food resources, probably on a seasonal basis. The continued importance of such food sources is demonstrated by a substantial shell midden, comprised almost entirely of limpets, at Sheader on Sandray, C14 dated to the mid-second millennium BC.

That the free-standing roundhouse continued in use through the Bronze Age, particularly in the many parts of our islands where there was no machair, seems certain however. Roundhouses spanning the late Bronze Age/early Iron Age transition have been excavated at Cladh Hallan on South Uist and we found remains of a similar if somewhat smaller house belonging to the same transitional period in the Borve valley. It may have been preceded by a similar house nearby, or even on the same site, for underneath it we found an area of cobbles flanked by a fine paved path (**27**) which had been well worn before it was overlain by a covered drain. The surrounding deposits yielded remains of several pottery vessels including flat-rimmed

27 The well-worn slabs of a Late Bronze Age paved path at site B54, Borve valley

buckets from the late Bronze Age/early Iron Age transition (**28**). The roundhouse immediately overlay these deposits, and although it had been partly destroyed by later lazy-bed cultivation, its main features could be identified (**29**). Its walls were stone-faced and packed with earth and over a metre wide. Its interior floor area was about 15m2, with a hearth area against its west wall, flanked by indications of a light internal partition of some kind. Fragments of pottery bowls from the floor deposit are of early Iron Age date.

This type of roundhouse clearly continued in use into at least the beginning of the Iron Age. At the moment our knowledge of the islands in the period from

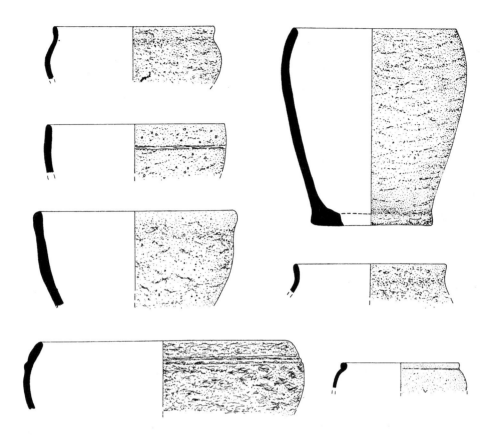

28 *LBA and EIA pottery from site B54, Borve valley. The earlier vessels, 5 and 6, are probably LBA/EIA transitional period and were associated with the paved path. The finer and more shapely bowls 13 and 15 are EIA and came from the overlying roundhouse*

some time before 2000 BC to around 500 BC is dominated by monuments associated with ritual action. The stone rings are few in number and seem likely therefore to have acted as ritual centres for groups of people spread over quite wide areas of the landscape. On Barra at least there is the possibility that each served as a ritual focus for its own segment of the island, but with Brevig perhaps being the pre-eminent centre to judge from its concentration of rings and standing stones. It is possible that the ring on south Vatersay served both Vatersay and Sandray, and that on Mingulay served also for Pabbay and Berneray, given that there is some evidence that all the islands (except possibly Berneray) were occupied in the Bronze Age. The burial cairns which are found on all the islands (again with the possible exception of Berneray) may have provided a more localised ritual or spiritual focus for much smaller groups of people – extended families or kin-groups perhaps. There is no evidence of ongoing or repeated ritual at the cairns, but we should not assume that they were necessarily either forgotten

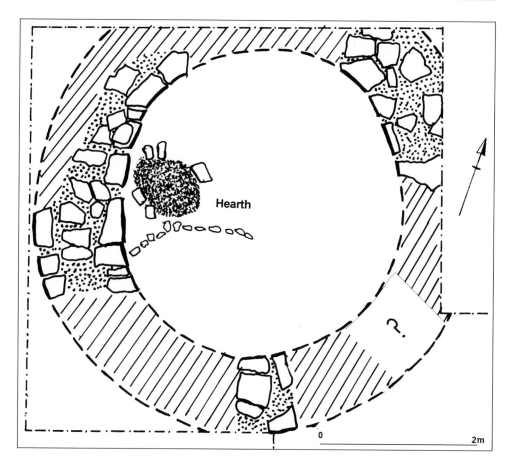

Hearth

29 Plan of the EIA roundhouse, B54, Borve valley. Much of the wall circuit had been destroyed by modern lazy-bed cultivation

or passive elements in the landscape; and according to our survey there were almost 100 of them spread through the islands, acting as ever-present memorials to the ancestors, and statements about the identity of the living.

4 Hierarchical landscapes

For many years the changes in patterns of settlement, types of settlement and settle-ment architecture, which appear to take place in the mid-first millennium BC in many parts of the British Isles, have been set in landscapes that were becoming increasingly bleak. The Iron Age, we have been told, was cold and wet and this was reflected in the natural fauna and flora, as well as in the retreat from upland areas, the pressure on good land in the lowlands, and the increase in levels of hostility between communities competing for the best of the available resources. Recent research in northern Britain, some of it by colleagues working on Barra and the Uists, has led to a serious revision of this scenario. Pollen studies and isotope analyses in particular have suggested that the Iron Age may have been no wetter or colder than preceding eras. This view is supported by the evidence for submerged Iron Age sites in lochs which suggests that the water level is higher today than it was 2000 years ago, and by the pattern of settlement that we have found in the islands in the period between about 500 BC and AD 500.

The settlement pattern in this period includes a multiplicity of site-types which certainly overlap in usage and in several instances appear to be largely contempora-neous. In the machair on Barra and the small area around the village bay on Mingulay there are remains of large middens associated in many cases with traces of disturbed stone structures. A few of these may be subterranean roundhouses of the types found in South Uist, where a hole is dug in the sand and lined with a stone skin, so that the wall of the house is only one stone wide. But the majority of identified occupa-tion sites of this period in the southern isles are free-standing, above ground struc-tures which have to be built in a different way.

The most prolific occupation sites are the thick-walled round and oval houses, which we have seen were already being constructed before the end of the Bronze Age. These houses fall into two groups according to their size, one group being between 8-12m and the other between 5-7m in overall diameter. About 40 of the smaller houses have been recorded and 35 of the larger.

The smaller houses are particularly problematic in terms of their dating. In truth we know that not all these houses belong in the Iron Age; the Beaker house at Alt Chrisal was a thick-walled roundhouse about 4.5m diameter, while an oval house described in the next chapter is probably of Norse date. That the type was also used into the Iron Age is certain, because we have already described at the end of the last chapter a circular house with late Bronze Age/early Iron Age pottery. Another house, on Vatersay, has yielded three probably middle Iron Age sherds from a rabbit burrow, but this house was markedly oval (6 x 4.5m). The rest of our small round-

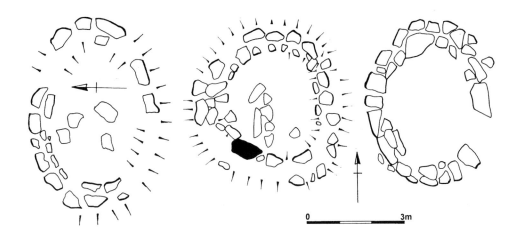

0 _____ 3m

*30 Three small oval or round huts found in survey on Barra. This type of structure was
built and used from the neolithic to the post-medieval period and is difficult to date from
surface remains alone. At least two examples have yielded Iron Age pottery*

houses are known only from surface remains, with no associated cultural material
(**30**). On the basis of the four examples with some dating evidence one might tentatively suggest that the oval houses are more likely to be Iron Age or early medieval,
but excavation of several more examples would be needed to strengthen this suggestion. Nevertheless, it seems certain that some of the smaller round and oval houses
are Iron Age.

The majority of the smaller houses (70 per cent) are in fact oval rather than round,
and on average they are about 40 per cent longer than they are wide. They have
stone-faced walls with an earth core, but we suspect that the upper parts of the walls
may often have been built in turf and were therefore probably rebuilt many times
during their occupation. They provide a living space which varies from as little as
7m^2 up to 20m^2.

About half of the houses are found over 100m above sea level, and several are
above the 150m contour. Their small size, taken together with their location, might
suggest that these houses were in fact seasonal shieling huts, used in the summer
months when the cattle were taken up to higher pastures. But we are not convinced
that this was so. There are many similar huts found in low-lying situations, and there
are numerous smaller huts and shelters (2-4m diameter) on the uplands which are
probably shieling huts, although they remain undated. But we also find that the larger
roundhouses, almost certainly permanently occupied, are very similarly distributed
between lowland and upland locations.

The larger roundhouses, between 8m and 12m diameter, include three which
have been sampled by excavation and produced Middle Iron Age pottery, and a
fourth which has yielded sherds of similar material from rabbit disturbance, so we
are more confident about the attribution of these houses to an Iron Age date.

31 A large roundhouse, twice reoccupied and modified, on Mingulay (MY344). The foundations of the original house, 12m in diameter, can be traced beneath the later walling

Their walls vary from 1-1.5m in width, and again are stone-faced with an earth core. In a few rare cases subsequent reuse and modification of the structure have led to their survival as standing structures (**31**). Mostly, however, their remains are marked by appreciable amounts of collapsed stonework. This is often insufficient to suggest they were necessarily completely built in stone, although we know many have been used as 'quarries' for later walls and shielings (**32**). The sampling excavations on two houses on the Tangaval peninsula on Barra, and a third in Mingulay Bay (**colour plate 21**), provided little insight into the interior arrangement of the houses, but a late Bronze Age/early Iron Age transitional house of this sort was completely excavated by our colleague Mike Parker Pearson on South Uist.

This house had an overall diameter of about 8m, and was entered by a door facing to the east. The floor was covered with compacted peat-ash spread from a hearth area near, but not at, the centre of the living space. There were no substantial interior divisions, although post-holes and stake-holes may indicate the position of at least one wattle screen.

We can reasonably assume that the houses on Barra and Vatersay were similar inside. These houses obviously provide much more living space than the small roundhouses, with between 30m² and 70m² of floor space. This would allow for areas to be set aside for different functions – sleeping, eating, food preparation – or for larger numbers of occupants, but there is no clear evidence for either at present.

32 A large roundhouse (B44), overlain by two shieling huts. The 12m diameter circuit wall, almost totally turf-covered, can be best seen at the left of the photo

But if the small houses and the large houses are broadly contemporary, as we believe, then the marked difference in the size of the houses and the living space they offered is presumably indicative of differences in either the resources and probably the status of the occupants, or in the size of the social group which the buildings housed.

These large roundhouses, like the small ones, are found in a wide variety of locations. A few are found within 30m of the sea, others are further inland but just above the valley floor and close to a stream, like an example in Skipisdale on Mingulay. Some of the houses are on high plateaux 100–150m above sea level, like that between Ben Cliad and Ben Vaslain in north Barra. Two examples are found perched, one on a shelf against a rock face and another on the steep slope just below, either side of the 200m contour to the west of Heaval. Their size and the considerable investment of energy in their construction suggest that these are permanent homes, and their different locations suggest that they were supported by a variety of subsistence strategies, varying from the exploitation of seafood resources, to small-scale cultivation of crops and cattle raising, to heavy dependence on sheep and goat.

The roundhouse at Alt Chrisal was a particularly important discovery because it was found, albeit heavily robbed-out for its building stone, underlying another

33 The wheelhouse at Alt Chrisal after excavation; the original entrance is on the far, southern, side

circular stone building. This was a far more complex structure of a type well known in the Western Isles, and usually called a wheelhouse (**33**). The Alt Chrisal house had a circuit wall about 9m diameter overall, but its 1.4m thick wall, built of unhewn blocks of Lewisian gneiss, reduced the interior space to about 40m², slightly smaller than the building it overlay. And the use of this space was further constrained by the way in which it was divided into six cells, around a central area just 3.5m in diameter, by seven free-standing stone piers (**34**). Since the central area was occupied by a hearth more than 2m square, framed by stone blocks, movement around the inside of the house must have been mainly along the narrow 'aisle' between the piers and the circuit wall. This aisle could be accessed immediately one entered the house through the south-facing doorway. Little was found in the individual cells to help identify any variations in their use. Two small pits were found in two cells towards the rear of the house, and over 90 per cent of the pottery from inside the house was found in cell F to the right of the entrance, but as usual in the Barra soils no animal bones survived and cereal remains were spread thinly and apparently indiscriminately.

A similar wheelhouse to Alt Chrisal, excavated many years ago in Allasdale, 6km to the north (**35**), also had one cell in which a large quantity of pottery was found, including a large storage jar, together with charcoal from willow twigs,

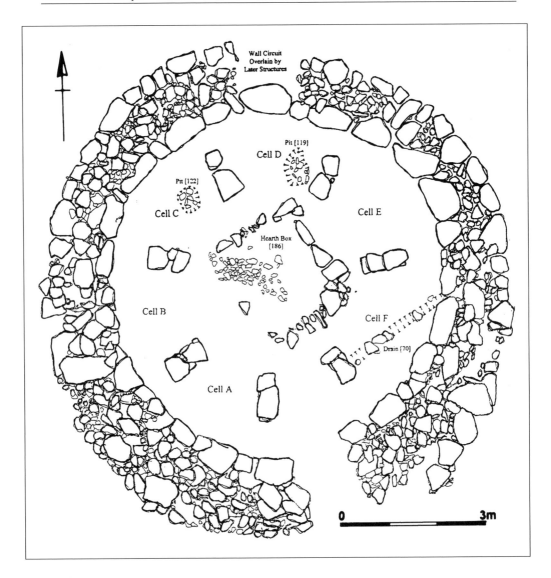

Wall Circuit
Overlain by
Later Structures

Pit [119]

Cell D

Pit [122]

Cell C

Cell E

Hearth Box
[186]

Cell B

Cell F

Cell A

Drain [70]

0   3m

34 The Alt Chrisal wheelhouse as first built, with a perimeter aisle

thought to be the remains of baskets, as this cell may have been a store or pantry. Other cells must certainly have been used for sleeping areas, and the piers obviously allowed for the possibility of segregating the members of the household by age or sex. The central hearth was clearly the unifying focus of household life, however, and at both Alt Chrisal and Allasdale mounds of ash, overspilling the stone kerb, conjured up pictures of roaring fires around which the family clustered on long, stormy winter nights.

Because the piers have such a dominant influence on the use of space within a wheelhouse, and are so eye-catching on the published plans of these houses, it is

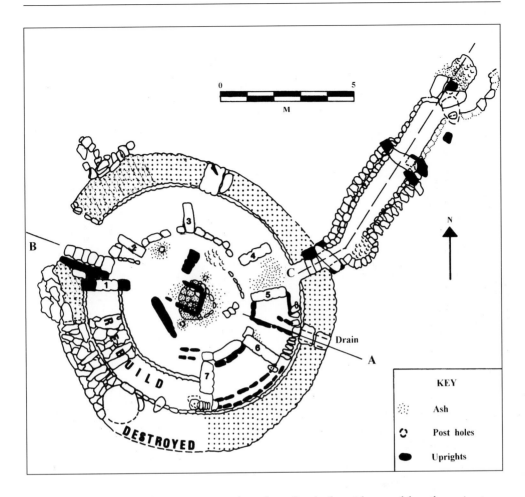

35 The Allasdale wheelhouse as it may have been first built, with central hearth, perimeter drain, and souterrain

not surprising that archaeologists have spent much time discussing both the practical purpose of the piers as space dividers and also their symbolic values. There is also the intriguing question as to whether the extension of the piers to meet the perimeter wall and block the aisle, thus making each cell self-contained (**36**), as happened in several houses including Alt Chrisal, reflected changing social behaviour. But the piers certainly had an important functional purpose too. In a landscape long since devoid of most trees, building roofs to span diameters of 7–10m presented major problems, and one way to get around them was to shorten the span over the central areas by building piers. Although we found no evidence *in situ* at Alt Chrisal, long stone slabs that were probably lintels were recovered, and we know from other wheelhouses in the Western Isles that piers were linked together by lintel stones, and they were also tied to the circuit wall by paired lintels. The cells and the aisle were then roofed by corbelled stone roofing, leaving just the

36 The blocking between pier 6 and the perimeter wall, Alt Chrisal wheelhouse. Note the thick deposit which built up in the aisle, alongside the pier, before the blocking was inserted

central area – perhaps only 4-5m diameter at most – to be covered with a roof supported on timbers. At Allasdale charred material, perhaps from heather, was found collapsed over the central area and was thought to be roof covering, supported perhaps on spruce poles, for which charcoal evidence was found. Although the aisle may have had a ceiling little more than 1.3m above the floor, the cells' corbelled ceilings may have been more than 2m high (well above head-height for the inhabitants) and the roof over the central area may have risen well over 4m above the hearth.

The wheelhouses on Barra and its neighbouring islands would therefore have been quite prominent in the landscape, because almost all of the 20 identified examples were free-standing structures, unlike the subterranean wheelhouses on the Uists and Lewis and Harris. These houses were dug down into the soft sands of the machair, and by definition therefore were mostly found close to the sea in low-lying situations. Whilst some of the wheelhouses in the southern isles, including Alt Chrisal, are found within 100m of the coastline, others are found 2-3km from the coast – about as far from the sea as its possible to get on an island the size of Barra. And like the small and large simple roundhouses, they are sometimes found in the high upland pastures 150-200m above sea level (**colour plate 22**). Their appearance at these altitudes reinforces the argument that people

37 The dominant and defensible site of Dun Scurrival, Barra, which overlooks the hill pasture, the machair, and the beaches of Eoligarry

were living permanently in these locations in the Middle Iron Age, for no one has suggested that wheelhouses were merely glorified shieling huts.

Impressive as they were, however, in terms of visual dominance they were outshone, just as they were overlooked, by the so-called 'true brochs' or broch towers, which at their best rose 10-15m high. None of the Western Isle brochs survive to their full height, and most are reduced to their bottom 2-3m (**colour plate 23**), but their double concentric walls separated by a 'gallery' are often clearly visible and betray their true nature. There are at least eight such structures in the southern isles, with single examples on Pabbay, Sandray and Vatersay, and the remainder on Barra. There are another half-dozen sites which *might* be brochs, but on present surface evidence these, although related, could be variant structures. Of these the most intriguing is Dun Scurrival, sitting in a dominant position overlooking most of the Eoligarry peninsula (**37**). Traces of an outer wall, inner wall and gallery can be seen along with masses of tumbled masonry. But it is somewhere between oval and pear-shaped and is not easily reconstructed as a broch tower. The eight brochs of which we are confident vary in overall size from 15-22m in diameter, so the amount of space they occupy is considerably greater than that of the largest wheelhouses and simple roundhouses.

However, much of this space is occupied by walling, because the broch towers have two concentric walls, each of which is 0.8-1.8m wide, separated by a narrow space 0.6-0.8m wide. The central spaces of most of the brochs therefore were a little larger, and in some cases slightly smaller, than those of the largest of the simple roundhouses. However it would be rash to assume that the amount of living space was no greater. Brochs which survive to any appreciable height invariably have scarcement ledges to support at least one upper floor, and the galleries have one or two floors above ground level. There is usually evidence of stairs in the gallery which provide access to the upper floor. The upper floor, presumably of wood, probably served as the main living area in a broch tower. This is suggested not only by the absence of evidence for substantial hearths on the ground floors of many brochs, but also by the very uneven floor surfaces. In the one, largely destroyed, broch that we excavated, on the isle of Pabbay the bedrock dipped alarmingly into an irregular hollow or pit. The surviving ground floors of the brochs may therefore have been the equivalent of a basement or cellar and were perhaps used in the same way, for storage and for craft activity or food processing. Corbelled chambers built into the double wall and sometimes given paved floors, as on Pabbay, provided additional, isolated storage cells.

The galleries meanwhile provided not only access to the floor or floors above, but also a means of air circulation and perhaps even light-wells to allow at least some daylight to percolate into these otherwise dark central rooms. The galleries were floored (or roofed – depending which way you look at them) with large slab-like stones set across between the two main walls. These gallery slabs can still be seen at several of the brochs in the southern isles, most notably at Dun Caolis on Vatersay. Further slabs were used to build stairs linking the successive galleries together, and providing access to the roof. This must have been built on a wooden framework like that used in the wheelhouses, but will have needed much longer timbers to bridge a central area of 9-13m in diameter.

From the top of a broch tower, the views must in some cases have been quite spectacular and probably always included a view of the sea. Some brochs like Dun Ban and Dun na Kille on the west coast of Barra, and Dunan Ruadh on Pabbay (**38**), are on headlands which see majestic Atlantic seas breaking against them. Dun Clieff, if it is a true broch, perches on a tiny tidal islet constantly hammered by Atlantic rollers (**colour plate 24**). There is almost a degree of bravado in the placing of these broch towers. Others, like Baigh Hirivagh (**colour plate 25**) and Dun Loch nic Ruaidhe on eastern Barra, sit on islets in a sheltered sea-loch or an inland freshwater loch, both protected and accessed by a stone causeway. Dun Caolis on Vatersay and Dun Cuier on Barra sit atop steep-sided but relatively low hills, less than 50m above sea level and within 400m of the sea. But both of these brochs exercised important vantage points. Dun Caolis overlooked both the east and west coasts, and the Sound of Vatersay, as well as the local machair, whilst Dun Cuier overlooked the west coast, the extensive machair to the west and north, and the whole of Allasdale and the pass to the east coast of the island. The most dramatic location is that of Dun Sandray (**colour plate 6**), perched on a rocky crag 170m above sea level, overlooking a fertile valley, a freshwater loch covered with pink flowers, and a view down the island chain to Barra Head. Caught early on a misty morning it is a literally magical sight, at least to a romantic archaeologist!

The occupants of Dun Sandray could no doubt have seen the walls of another hilltop structure at Barra Head on Berneray, standing in a suicidal position on the

38 Dunan Ruadh on its exposed rocky headland, Pabbay. Only about 20 per cent of its massive wall foundation had survived the Atlantic storms

edge of the 180m high cliffs, now occupied by the nineteenth-century lighthouse. This structure has been largely destroyed by the quarrying of its stone for the lighthouse, but sufficient survives to recognise it as a close relative of the broch towers. It had a double wall, with internal galleries, and according to Miss Isabella Bird who saw it in 1863, it still stood about 30ft high. Although this may have been an optimistic estimate, there is no doubt that this wall stood tall (another visitor in 1890 put it then at 13ft) and that it was a truly monumental structure. Even in the reduced remains that survive today, the largest blocks of stone used in the wall are up to 2m long.

Unlike the brochs, however, the Barra Head structure did not form a complete circuit. Its massive strength was displayed in the only direction from which it could be approached – uphill, from the east-facing slope of the island. To protect the inhabitants from the fearsome winds, and the perpendicular drop to the ocean far beneath, there appears to have been a much lower and thinner wall along the cliff-top. Indeed we must wonder whether this hill-top stronghold was ever permanently inhabited or whether it formed a retreat to which one could flee in the event of a hostile raid from the sea. About 400m to the north another headland was enclosed by a low double-faced stone wall. Although the site is known as Dun Briste and might be called a promontory fort, both terms are misleading. There is nothing to suggest that the wall ever stood much higher than 1.5-2m, nor that there were any contemporary houses within it. It was probably a safe enclosure where livestock belonging to the users of the galleried dun could be penned. A similar enclosure is found on the neighbouring island of Mingulay, also perched atop dramatic cliffs and known as Dun Mingulay. It too reveals no evidence of monumentality or human occupation in the past, and is best viewed as another livestock enclosure.

A third 'promontory fort', found on the little island of Biruaslum, separated from the island of Vatersay by a vertical sea-dyke, is a very different structure. Here there is an impressive stone wall, built of quite regular blocks of stone, still standing 3m high and 2m wide. It runs in an arc for a distance of about 100m, before it anchors itself against a rocky outcrop. There is an entrance about 2.5m wide at the highest point of the arc. The wall is apparently built to defend an area of land immediately adjacent to Vatersay from attack from the sea, via the west coast of Biruaslum; defence from an attack from Vatersay itself is provided by the sea-dyke. The only dating evidence recovered inside the wall comes from a midden being eroded by the sea, which yielded five pieces of flint and five sherds, the most diagnostic of which is from a Neolithic bowl. Despite this evidence, this type of structure is best paralleled by promontory forts of the first millennium AD, and it recalls, albeit on a more modest scale, the cliff-forts of Cahercommaun in Co. Clare and Dun Aongusa in Galway.

The building of the walls of the 'promontory forts', whether as defences or simply enclosures, is the first evidence we can firmly identify on the islands for the erection of linear structures running for distances of 20-100m. We suspect that walls to enclose cultivation plots had been built much earlier, but at present we have no evidence for them. But we believe there may be other stretches of walling that we can tentatively date to the Iron Age and relate in at least two instances to occupation sites. One of these is a linear bank that runs across Borve headland from the edge of the sea heading straight towards the broch which now sits in the corner of the nineteenth-century cemetery. At its terminal point on the headland, the bank divides into two and forms two sides of a triangle, the third side now being formed by the invading sea. Sitting on the bank which makes up this triangular enclosure are a series of spaced upright stones. We have noticed a similar type of boundary, which we call 'monolith on bank' on Vatersay, around the broch of Dun Caolis. Here, the banks not only appear to form a radial pattern from the hill on which the broch stands, but their antiquity is suggested by the way a bank disappears beneath bog and re-emerges 20-30m further on. Sounding confirms that the bank continues beneath the bog. A similar length of bank which disappears into a bog and re-emerges further on was found on Sandray about 200m from a large roundhouse. 'Monolith on bank' boundaries are found in more isolated positions elsewhere on Barra and in one location in the Borve valley we found a sub-rectangular hut of *c.*AD 1700 that had been built over the remains of such a bank. Dating these boundaries is extremely difficult, but we think that fragments of Iron Age boundary systems do survive.

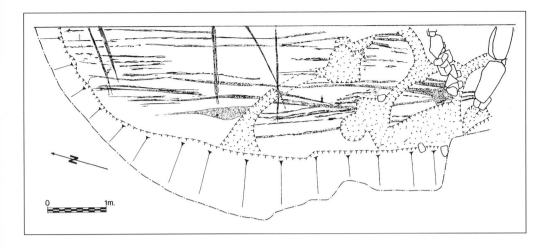

39 Iron Age plough marks left in the sandy spoil beneath a roundhouse on Mingulay. They are the results of one-way rather than cross-ploughing

The purpose of such boundaries may have been partly to mark out territory but also to enclose cultivated plots and to control livestock. Direct evidence of cultivated land was found on the ground surface sealed beneath the Mingulay roundhouse. Within the small area excavated (10 x 2m) there were about 25 north-south plough marks left in the subsoil, and five which ran roughly east-west (**39**). This suggests that the tradition of cross-ploughing found in neolithic and Bronze Age fields further south in Britain was not followed, or had been abandoned by the Middle Iron Age, in this part of the Outer Hebrides. Many of the marks ran for only 2-4m, and the longest for only 6m, and it may be that the simple wooden plough that made these marks was pulled by human rather than animal traction. This particular cultivated area was on machair, where the soils were light, well-drained and easy to plough. But elsewhere ploughing may have been difficult if not impossible. Weeds found in samples taken from the wheelhouse at Alt Chrisal suggest that the inhabitants of this farmstead were cultivating wetter, heavier peatland – which is the only land available to this site. Such land, on a steepish slope and strewn with stones and boulders, would have required a lot of hard labour to crop it year after year. It would probably have to be turned over with spades rather than ploughs, and would need to be manured either with dung or with seaweed, laboriously dragged from the rocky coast of the Sound of Vatersay. Over time, the soil would become increasingly thin, wet and patchy.

The only crop being sown in these cultivated plots or small fields was still six-row hulled barley, remains of which were found in the simple roundhouse and the overlying wheelhouse at Alt Chrisal and in the Pabbay broch. Although rotary querns appeared further north in the island chain in the last centuries BC, we have no examples from prehistoric sites in the southern isles and a Middle Iron Age quern from the platform outside Scurrival cave was a very basic 'saucer' quern.

Stone rubbers, probably used on saucer or saddle querns to grind the grain to flour, were found on all the excavated sites.

Given the difficulty of growing crops, animal husbandry, hunting and fishing must have provided the bulk of the food consumed by the Iron Age population of our islands. The later prehistoric exploitation of animal resources is better evidenced than that of earlier prehistory thanks to excavations on sand-based soils on Mingulay and Sandray, two small soundings in similar soils by the Borve broch and the Scurrival cave, and the preservation of remains in a pit in the broch on Pabbay. Animal bones were recovered from all of these deposits. The picture they present is remarkably uniform. Sheep account for about 80-85 per cent of the identified remains and cattle for about 10 per cent. Pig is found in all the deposits but in very low numbers – rarely above one per cent. Other domesticated animals are not found but for a single instance of horse, and indirect evidence of dog. The remainder of the mammal bones are from Atlantic and Common seal, and occasional red deer and whale.

The dominance of sheep is unsurprising anywhere in the Outer Hebrides, but they are more numerous in the southern islands than on the Uists, where they represent 40-70 per cent of the domesticates found in wheelhouse contexts. This almost certainly reflects the very limited areas of good machair grazing available in the southern isles, and the extensive areas of upland suitable only for rough sheep pasture. The shortage of good grazing equally explains the much lower levels of cattle stocking on our islands, which contrast with the evidence of the Uist wheelhouses, where they make up 25-55 per cent of domesticates. The lower numbers of pig in the southern islands, on the other hand, are not easily explained by environmental factors. While they were never a major component of the bone assemblages from the Uist wheelhouses, where they commonly make up 3-10 per cent of the domesticated stock, in the broch at Dun Vulan they represented 12 per cent of the bone assemblage, and deposits outside the broch gave even higher figures. In the Pabbay broch they barely represent one per cent of the animals. This most probably represents social and territorial rather than environmental factors. If, as is widely believed by Iron Age archaeologists, the consumption of pig was associated with feasting hosted by those of elite status, then the probable limitations of the territory and status of the occupants of the Pabbay broch may well be reflected in their food refuse.

All the animals – sheep, cattle and pig – were mostly killed off at a very young age. This again is a pattern common throughout the Hebrides, but it is perhaps particularly true on the smaller of our southern islands. The natural grazing resources of these islands were very limited and few animals could be maintained into adulthood and overwintered. The evidence from Pabbay, Mingulay and Sandray is such that the faunal specialist who examined the bones from these sites suggested that cattle may not have been reared on these islands at all, but brought in as calves from Barra or Vatersay. Similarly, it is suggested that the occasional eating of venison reflects not the hunting of animals on these islands (which were mostly too small to support and protect wild herds), but the infrequent acquisition of joints of venison from South Uist.

What Barra and its southern neighbours lacked in beef and pork, however, could be partly made up from bird and marine life. Bones of 22 species of birds were recovered from the Pabbay broch, and of five species from the Mingulay midden. Shag were by far the most prolific birds represented, and there is a Hebridean tradition of making soup with this bird. The other birds used in moderate numbers were the Manx Shearwater, Gulls, and Puffins. The occasional goose and duck must have been regarded as a welcome change of diet! Shell middens on Sandray, Pabbay, and at Eoligarry on Barra demonstrate that the age-old tradition of collecting cockles and limpets (and a variety of other shellfish in smaller numbers) was continued on all the islands during the Iron Age. Fish bones were found in all the deposits yielding animal bones, and not surprisingly the cod family (cod, saithe, pollack, ling) was the commonest in each group. In the Pabbay broch, however, sea bream were also very common, and conger eel and balan wrasse were notable contributors to the diet. All of these fish are inshore types which could have been caught either with lines from the shore, or with nets from small boats. The Atlantic seals could also have been easily acquired by waiting until the breeding season, when they come ashore. But the appearance of the common seal, in rather greater numbers than the Atlantic, suggests that some seals were caught at sea.

We have no direct evidence of the boats which were available to the people of the Hebrides at this time, but a gold model boat of the Iron Age from Broighter in northern Ireland shows a vessel with both a mast and oars. Given the close contacts between Ireland and the southern end of the Hebridean chain from early prehistory onwards, boats like this must have been known to the inhabitants of Barra and its neighbours, though smaller boats were presumably used for inshore fishing. It is possible that the boat represented by the Broighter model was made of skin, over a wooden frame. Roman sources mention their use in Britain and, although they look and sound too flimsy to have braved the Minches, a modern replica proved strong enough to cross the Atlantic. On the other hand the rocky landing sites which were all that many of our islands offered, and which had to be negotiated in a heavy swell, cannot have been easy for skin boats to use. Wooden hulls must have been preferable in these circumstances. Nevertheless, acquiring the wood to build even fishing boats must have been difficult on islands where few trees were any longer to be found, and the wood, or even the finished boats, probably had to be acquired by trade with people on the mainland. For a people with few natural resources at their command, this trade must have stretched their economy to its limits.

One product which might have proved exchangeable on the mainland was wool and woollen clothing. Because so many sheep were slaughtered young for their meat, the amount of wool that could be gathered from the breeding flock would have been limited. However, spindle-whorls from the wheelhouses at Allasdale and Alt Chrisal and from the Pabbay broch confirm that wool was collected and spun, and loomweights from both Allasdale and Alt Chrisal further confirm that it was woven into cloth. Preserved woollen garments from Denmark and Orkney show that in addition to leggings and jackets, shawls and hooded cloaks – ideal protection from the Hebridean winds – were in the Iron Age wardrobe. Bone toggles found at Dun Scurrival and Pabbay probably came from cloaks like these. Other clothing may have been made from leather and from seal-skin, and lumps of pumice with smoothed surfaces from Iron Age deposits at Balnabodach and Alt Chrisal may have been used in the cleaning of skins for this purpose. Bone awls found in the Pabbay broch and a bone needle and awl from Dun Cueir were presumably used primarily for making clothing too.

Bone and antler working were minor craft activities practised in the island households. The Pabbay broch yielded a range of simple practical tools and implements – awls, punches, a spatula, a spoon and a toggle probably used to fasten a cloak – all of which were presumably made on the spot. Pins were notably absent from the main period of occupation, a situation also noted in the broch at Dun Vulan on South Uist. The discovery of small crucibles in the Alt Chrisal wheelhouse, the Dun Cuier broch and the Pabbay broch, along with iron slag from both Dun Cuier and Pabbay, might suggest that small-scale metalworking was practised in these Iron Age households. There is some reason for thinking, however, that in each case this activity may relate to post-Iron Age occupation of these sites, and this evidence will be discussed further in the next chapter. Certainly, most of our Iron Age occupation sites continue to yield flint tools – knives and scrapers – in small numbers, which suggests that sparse supplies of iron tools had to be supplemented by the use of stone (and bone) implements which were still being made in the same way as 3000 years earlier.

Pottery too continued to be entirely hand-made, probably fired in turf clamps, and showing only hints of being influenced by styles and shapes from the world beyond. The larger vessels are mostly thick-walled bucket-like pots, presumably used mostly for storage. Cooking pots include globular jars with slightly closed rims, perhaps best used for hanging over a fire with soups or stews, and taller, more narrow-based jars which could have been stood in the ashes of a fire. A few simple bowls and dishes could have served as 'tableware' if such refinements were recognised. Given the rather coarse fabrics and unprepossessing shapes it is somewhat surprising to find such a wide variety of decoration on the pots (**40**). It is mostly incised into the pot's surface in the form of ladder patterns, 'christmas trees', hatched triangles, lattices, and multiple diagonal or vertical lines. A smaller numbers of pots have impressed decoration, most frequently on the rims where fingers or fingernails have been repeatedly pressed onto the top surface. But wood or bone points were also used to make lines or circles of impressed dots on the shoulders of vessels. A third form of decoration, found mostly on the neck or shoulder of large jars is the applied cordon of clay, usually pinched from alternate sides to make a raised wavy band running around the pot. Although the pots from different sites share this repertoire of motifs, it is noticeable how idiosyncratic the detail of the decoration can be and how often a site produces a few motifs not found elsewhere. It seems likely that each household or each group of households made its own pots.

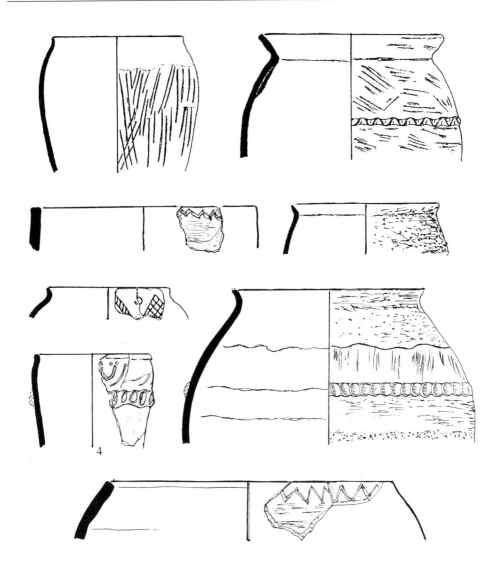

40 Iron Age pottery from Dunan Ruadh, Pabbay. Decoration is quite common, mostly incised in chevron patterns, hatched cordons and triangles, or groups of diagonal lines. The finger-impressed clay cordon is also popular

In fact the overwhelming impression from the cultural material found in the roundhouses, wheelhouses and brochs is one of self-sufficiency. Very little was obtained by exchange with the world outside the islands. The occasional item of bronze or iron (like the fragmentary brooch and fragments of knives from Allasdale wheelhouse), and a few pieces of simple jewellery (coloured beads from Allasdale or a shale bangle from Alt Chrisal) seem to be the only personal items acquired from across the seas. There may have been others of wood, such as furniture or

But what about the brochs? The pottery from the Pabbay broch has been compared to that from the Sollas wheelhouse in North Uist, which C14 dating places in the first or second century AD. The earliest pottery from Dun Cuier is also middle Iron Age. Dun Vulan on South Uist is C14 dated to the first or second century BC, earlier in the middle Iron Age. With some other Hebridean wheel-houses producing C14 dates in the last centuries BC, it seems that brochs and wheelhouses were indeed contemporaries in the landscape. In the period *c*.200BC –200AD therefore we may have had a landscape in which brochs, wheelhouses and some of the large and small simple roundhouses could all be seen.In terms of size and the mobilisation of resources that they represent they seem to form a hierarchy.

These various monuments also form clusters in some areas on Barra. For example in Allasdale we find three large roundhouses and a probable wheelhouse within 400m of each other; in Borve a wheelhouse and three small roundhouses stand within 500m; above Glen a wheelhouse, a large roundhouse, and two small ones are within 300m; and in Gortein a probable wheelhouse, large roundhouse and two small roundhouses are spread over 400m. On Vatersay, above the old schoolhouse, a wheelhouse, two large and one small roundhouse stand within 300m. Further along the same slope three large roundhouses and two small ones cluster within 250m. The biggest cluster of all is around Tresivick, where over a distance of about 600m there are two wheelhouses, four large roundhouses, three small roundhouses and a huge grassed over mound that might hide a broch. An important point at all of these sites is that there is no obvious signs that some buildings have been demolished or robbed to provide stone for others, as one might expect if the remains represented a sequence of buildings. That is, the evidence of the surface remains does not conflict with the limited evidence from the excavated sites, and suggests that most of these different types of houses were at least partly contemporary.

Given that these clusters are often surrounded by considerable areas with no trace of other permanent occupation sites, they seem to reflect a deliberate decision of the households that occupied the various buildings to live in close proximity. Since the clusters are mostly not found in defensive locations, and since they are not grouped so tightly that they offered mutual security, or strength in numbers, we believe that they probably represent social clusters, perhaps of extended families or kin-groups. In that case, the hierarchy that the various houses represent would be one of status rather than power as such. The head of the kin-group might live in a broch which the whole group had helped to build and which could act as a refuge for everyone in times of hostilities. Other senior families in the kin-group – those perhaps of the head's siblings – might occupy wheelhouses, while families lower in the kin-group hierarchy lived in large simple roundhouses. The smaller roundhouses might be occupied by unmarried or lone adults, or be used for various seasonal purposes and activities.

This reconstruction of a landscape which essentially reflects local social hierarchies is, of course, entirely speculative. But it fits the observed pattern of settlement with its mixed clusters of buildings, at least as well as any other interpretation that has been offered. It provides a framework within which the mobilisation of manpower for building a broch might be understood without recourse to models involving 'elites' whose basis of power is unclear. Taken together with topography it also provides a possible 'social' map of Barra with six or seven natural catchments each occupied by a kin-group numbering 30-60 people, making up an island population of perhaps 200-400 inhabitants.

If that is anywhere near correct, it was surely the highest population that Barra had had since the first settlers reached the island in 3500 BC, and perhaps higher than it would boast again for almost another millennium.

5 Lost landscapes

Whatever the social basis of the island landscapes in the first two or three centuries AD, it is clear that significant changes were taking place by the end of this period. Brochs and wheelhouses were beginning to fall into disrepair and in some cases were no longer occupied. The number of sites with pottery or other cultural material that one can ascribe even approximate dates to also drops markedly, and since there is no evidence of nucleation of population into fewer, larger settlements it seems likely that the population was declining. Why this should be we do not know, but the impression is that a decline in population was accompanied by the break up of the social hierarchies and kinship communities of the period c.200 BC to AD 200.

Two contemporary processes which probably had nothing to do with either the falling population or the internal social collapse nevertheless may have contributed indirectly to the new socio-political configurations which emerged in the fourth and fifth centuries. The first was the withdrawal of Roman forces from southern Scotland, followed of course by their total withdrawal from Britain at the beginning of the fifth century. This left a political hiatus in, among other areas, south-west Scotland, and into it moved an Irish people, the Dalriada. They established a kingdom centred on Argyll and became known as the Scoti or Scots. Their arrival and expansion in turn put pressure on the indigenous peoples to form their own power-groups to oppose the invaders, and gradually a Pictish kingdom emerged which held sway over northern Scotland from the Western Isles across to the east coast. Only slowly, and unevenly, did anything approaching a 'Pictish' material culture begin to emerge and this has made the identification of 'Pictish' settlements and monuments particularly difficult. As a result, for many years Pictish landscapes have been lost to us, and the Picts have even appeared to be people without homes!

Nevertheless, recent excavations and reappraisals of previous ones have begun to identify continued occupation of the site of earlier wheelhouses and brochs in much simpler and less conspicuous buildings. Occupation continued within the existing buildings but in a radically altered form. The new buildings were constructed within the shell of the original structure and usually took the form of a large cellular room with a floor level below the level of the often reduced reused wall circuit. Small additional cells were often added and some of the architectural features of the earlier buildings were reused and seamlessly incorporated. Architecturally, these structures may be considered farmsteads rather than statements of status or wealth.

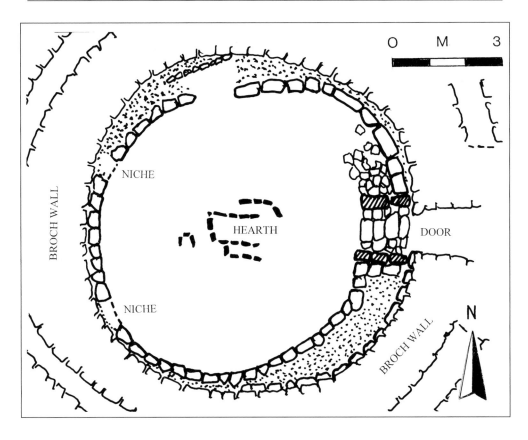

42 The Pictish cellular building in the shell of Dun Cueir. It has only been recognised as such long after the original excavations, which appear never to have reached the original Middle Iron Age deposits

At Cnip and Loch na Berie on Lewis, Edinburgh archaeologists recognised cellular structures built into the ruins of a wheelhouse and broch respectively. This picture is repeated on South Uist at Dun Vulan, and again on Barra. At Dun Cuier a cellular building was constructed inside the wall of the broch and on a clean layer of sand which was laid down to cover and level the debris of the earlier occupation (**42**). A rectangular stone-lined hearth was built in the middle of the floor. The plain undecorated pottery, mostly bucket-like storage pots (**43**) and a decorated composite comb suggest this structure was in use in the sixth and seventh centuries AD. At Alt Chrisal broadly contemporary occupation can be identified in the form of a series of temporary hearths and a rectilinear stone-lined hearth 1.3 x 1m in size, all located within the circuit wall of the wheelhouse, and associated with sherds from plain globular pots. A leaf-shaped socketed iron spearhead found associated with the hearth is of a type found in the fifth and sixth centuries AD.

Further south on Pabbay, the surviving fragment of the broch of Dunan Ruadh reveals late internal walls which appear to be traces of a cellular structure incorporating

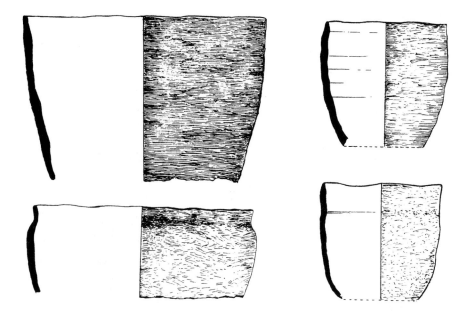

43 Pictish pottery from the reoccupation of Dun Cueir. These plain, heavy storage jars often with internal ridging are similar to vessels found in a cellular building inserted into the ruins of Dun Vulan on South Uist. After A. Young

one of the old wall chambers. A small associated midden yielded a bronze hand-pin with three 'fingers' along the top of the shield-like palm suggesting a sixth- or seventh-century date (**44**). A similar pin, longer and enamelled, and probably of seventh-century date, was found by a crofter around 1900 in a midden in the dunes west of the broch.

We suspect that many other earlier Iron Age occupation sites continued to be used in modified forms during the Pictish period but without careful excavation and detailed study of the material culture recognising them will be difficult. As for sites newly occupied in this period, they may well be found only by chance, and the one example we have discovered in the islands was indeed a fortuitous accident. In 1999 we noted the remains of two, possibly three, small circular huts inside a modern sheep pen on the slopes behind Northbay School. They sat above, and about 50m from, a stream overlooking the western end of Loch Obe. In size and location they reminded us of the two late neolithic huts we had excavated at Alt Chrisal, and as part of our detailed study of the evolution of human settlement around Loch Obe we decided to excavate one of them.

It proved to be a simple structure, with a stone wall about 70cm wide, revetted against a rocky outcrop, enclosing an area 2m in diameter (**45**). A gap in the stonework on the southern side denoted an entrance just 40cm wide. To the right of the door on entering, there appears to have been a low bench of turf, about

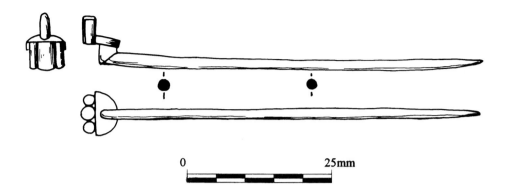

0   25mm

44 A Pictish bronze hand-pin from Dunan Ruadh, Pabbay. Two of these rare pins have been found on Pabbay

45 A Pictish shieling hut overlooking Loch Obe, Barra. Too small for permanent occupation, it did not even have any obvious hearth; cooking must have been done outside

30cm wide and just under 2m long. There were no other structural features in the hut, and in particular no hearth or fireplace. From the trodden earth floor we recovered twelve sherds of pottery, half of which were very small and weathered. Another sherd appeared to be neolithic in date, and the remaining five came from five different vessels. All of these were undecorated and two were made by the tongue-and-groove method of pot-building which is common in the Pictish period. Together with the absence of any flint material, which we have found in small quantities on all our excavated Iron Age sites, we believe the balance of the limited evidence points to a Pictish date for the hut's use.

The small size of the hut and the absence of a hearth of any kind, together with the one or two similar huts nearby, suggest this was the site of a temporary summer encampment used by shepherds, perhaps coming from the vicinity of Dun Cueir which is only two miles to the west.

Despite the unimpressive structural remains which are all the evidence we have for the homes of the islanders in this 'Pictish' period, their material culture at times seems more varied and interesting than that of the preceding era. The late reoccupation levels at Alt Chrisal wheelhouse, Dun Cuier and the Pabbay broch all produced remains of small metalworking crucibles probably involved in re-melting copper alloys. There was also part of an open mould at Dun Cuier, whilst Pabbay yielded lumps of iron slag. Whether the two bronze hand-pins from Pabbay and the iron spearhead from Alt Chrisal were local products is uncertain. If not, then their acquisition is all the more interesting, implying exchange contacts were maintained, perhaps even expanded, during the Pictish period. At Dun Cuier, however, it is bonework rather than metalwork that catches the eye (**46**). The high-backed composite comb mentioned earlier was accompanied by three other combs in various stages of completeness. There were also six bone dice from the excavations, and although some have suggested they are of earlier, Iron Age, date, there are mid-first-millennium dice of this type and they seem more likely to belong with the bulk of the pottery and the bone combs. The many bone pins and a needle from Dun Cuier (**47**) are matched by the proliferation of bone pins in Pictish levels at Dun Vulan (South Uist). Bonework from the Pabbay broch was simpler but included a knife handle and four pieces of worked antler. Again, the red deer antler is of interest because the nearest likely source of such material in the mid-first millennium AD was South Uist, and the material was probably acquired by barter and exchange.

Just what the Pictish period inhabitants of Pabbay had to exchange that the people of Uist might want is hard to imagine. The animal bones found in the midden associated with the fragmentary cellular structure inside the broch show that there was little change in the subsistence economy from the main period of the broch's usage, with sheep remaining the dominant animal. Cattle may have been slightly more important now than previously, but pigs were very few in number. There may have been more emphasis on fish in the diet during this period, with saithe and red sea bream the most common species. In general the subsistence economy of Pabbay remains somewhat impoverished if compared to the islands further north, and it is unlikely there were any food stuffs to exchange for imported materials.

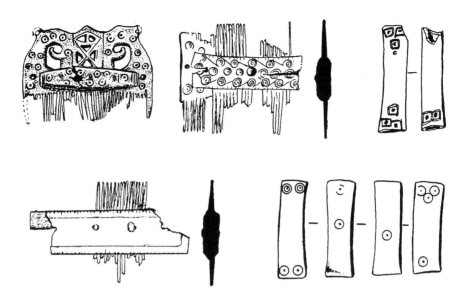

46 Bone combs and dice from the reoccupation of Dun Cueir: altogether pieces of four combs and six dice were found. After A. Young

In this context it is surprising to find on Pabbay a rare example in the Western Isles of a Pictish symbol stone (**colour plate 26**). These engraved stone slabs are numerous in north-east Scotland and several occur in Orkney and Shetland, but they are rarely found in the west, and only one other example is recorded from the Outer Hebrides. The Pabbay stone shares with the handful of slabs from Skye the engraved combination of an inverted crescent and superimposed V-rod, but the significance and meaning of this shared symbol is unknown. Indeed the original purpose and symbolism of the Pictish stones is also a mystery, since they are rarely found associated with archaeological sites. In that sense the Pabbay stone is of particular interest because it was found on a stone-clad mound of sand which was used as a cemetery at least some centuries later (**colour plate 27**). But the stone may have been taken from its original, probably sixth-century, location and context and reused as a grave marker, and the cross which is engraved standing on the top of the crescent may have been carved at that time. Nevertheless the Pabbay stone surely indicates that the Pictish inhabitants of the island were in some way incorporated into the social structures of the emergent Pictish kingdom.

It is possible that some Pictish burials were already being made in the stone-clad sand mound on which the stone was found, but the Picts also buried their dead in low, rectangular cairns with a stone kerb and a covering of pebbles or beach boulders. An example was recently excavated by our colleague Mike Parker Pearson at Kilpheder on South Uist and found to contain a central cist with the body of a woman about 40 years old, feet to the north and head turned to the west. The only

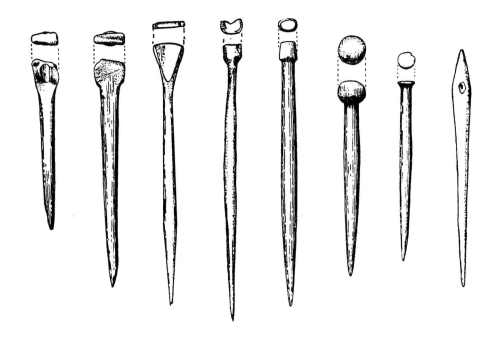

47 A selection of bone pins and a needle, from Dun Cueir. They were presumably made on site; the example on the left appears to be unfinished. After A. Young

grave good was a single pebble. Similar burials have been found on Lewis and on Berneray (in the Sound of Harris). We believe we may have located a couple of these low rectangular cairns on southern Sandray, only a short boat journey from Pabbay. Whether such cairns, if so they be, were the burial places of a Pictish family living on Sandray or whether Sandray was being used as a cemetery by the people living in Dunan Ruadh on Pabbay is open to speculation, but at present we have no other evidence of Pictish occupation on Sandray.

The very name of Pabbay, which means 'priest's island', and the modification of the Pictish symbol stone apparently to be used as a Christian grave marker raises the question as to when Christianity arrived in these islands. A bishopric had been established in south western Scotland in the fifth century, and in the mid-sixth century St Columba founded a monastery on Iona. It was this Celtic or Irish brand of Christianity that flourished in the north and west and was spread into the Western Isles by Columban monks. Concerned as it was with the immaterial rather than the material world, the early Celtic church founded monastic centres on remote islands and coastlines, of which the Hebrides has a surfeit.

There are no certain examples of early Celtic cashels or monastic enclosures in the Hebrides, but possible sites have been noted on Benbecula and South Uist, and a third at Kilbar at the northern end of Barra. The earliest surviving buildings here are almost certainly no earlier than the twelfth century, but most scholars who have studied this churchyard and its history believe it goes back into the pre-Norse (pre-late ninth-century) period. If the Norse named the island Barray after St Barr, to whom the church at Kilbar is dedicated, then it is argued that his church must already have been established here when they arrived. When he visited the site in 1816, McCulloch noted traces of a ditch around the churchyard which might be the remains of the cashel. Two small slabs with simple crosses on them might be early pre-Norse grave markers but there is no way to confirm this. Three such slabs, however, were found on the same stone-clad mound on Pabbay that produced the Christianised Pictish symbol stone. If the Norsemen called the island 'priests island' then it suggests that there was indeed a Christian settlement of some kind on Pabbay when the Norse first arrived here at the end of the ninth century. Similar stone-clad mounded cemeteries are known on Berneray and Mingulay, the former yielding another simple cross slab, but whether these cemeteries too go back to such an early period is unknown.

Pabbay, of course, is not exceptional in having a Norse place-name; indeed all of the six larger islands, and most of the smaller ones, that we have worked on have Norse names. Norse place-names dominate the Hebridean landscape even today; in Lewis it has been calculated that 99 per cent of all place-names are wholly or partly Norse in derivation. Such dominance inevitably suggests that the Western Isles were flooded with Viking invaders and settlers towards the end of the first millennium AD, and the sagas support that view. Following the violent raid on St Cuthbert's shrine at Lindisfarne monastery in AD 793, Viking raiders swept around the north and west coasts of Britain. The Hebrides were first raided in AD 795 and the raiders probably soon established temporary bases from which to conduct future raids further afield. This formative period is hazy in the historical records and almost invisible archaeologically. As temporary bases for bands of fighting men one might expect the sites to be small and ephemeral, but this is not necessarily the case. The crew of two Viking ships would alone number several dozen men, and form a bigger community than any of the known Pictish settlements could muster. And overwintering in the Western Isles would require substantial wind-proof housing of some kind to be built. But none of the handful of Norse period settlements so far found and explored in the Hebrides appears to belong to this very early raiding period, or to be the temporary homes of a group of warriors.

Although about three dozen Hebridean sites were identified by Alan Lane as yielding Norse pottery, in most cases only a few sherds of possible Norse type were identified and there was little or no information about the settlements in which they were used. Houses at the Udal in North Uist and Howmore in South Uist appeared to be isolated structures – the surviving fragments of a now lost Viking landscape. Recent work by Parker Pearson and Sharples on South Uist has demonstrated that in fact there were Norse settlements at frequent intervals along the machair. Excavations at Kilpheder have revealed a long sequence of successive houses occupied from the end of the tenth century to the mid-thirteenth. These houses are for the most part oblong structures with two opposing doorways, one in each long wall, and a central rectangular hearth area. They were built as essentially stone-lined pits in the sand, the upper and outer walls being of turf, long since gone. These houses are clearly different to the classic Viking house, and an adaptation to local conditions and materials.

It is possible that such structures and settlements remain to be found on Barra, Vatersay and the other southern islands. They are easily cloaked by the sand drifts of the machair, and in the dunes between Traigh Mhor and Traigh Eais on the Eoligarry peninsula, traces of middens with animal bones, shells, and pottery indicate hidden sites of some kind. But the pottery does not appear to be distinctively Viking. From one of these midden sites, however, came a small piece of decorated bronze sheet with an incised pattern which recalls the Norse Ringerike or Jellinge styles. Nevertheless this is slim evidence on which to repopulate this area of machair with Viking houses!

It may be that the small islands at the end of the Hebridean chain were not in fact used and settled by the Vikings in the same way that the Uists, Lewis and Harris were. According to a Norse saga, the first Viking to visit Barra was Onund Wooden Leg in AD 871. He arrived with five ships and remained on the island for three winters, using it as a base for summer raiding further south. Those Norse who followed him southwards may also have used these islands as a temporary base rather than a major settlement location. It has been noted that although Norse place-names abound on Barra and its islands, the vast majority of them are related to significant landmarks, especially those useful for coastal navigation. To mention a few examples, there are place-names for headlands ending in *nes* (e.g. Bruernish), for bays ending in *vagr* (e.g. Bagh Hirivagh) or *vik* (e.g. Brevig), for hills ending in *fjall* (e.g. Scurrival). Otherwise most Norse place-names in these islands refer to animal husbandry. Tangusdale, Allasdale and Eorisdale, for example, are *stodhull* – milking places – and names like Earsary and Skallary refer to an *erg* – a shieling or temporary summer camp. It is suggested that the place-names reflect a Norse presence which was not focused mainly on permanent settlement but on raiding abroad and with a thinly occupied landscape used for cattle raising. The only occupation sites of the Norse yet discovered and excavated on Barra support this view.

The more interesting is perhaps an oval hut found on the southern slopes of Ben Gunnary – Gunnar's Shieling as the Norse called it (**48**). It was a thick-walled oval hut, with external dimensions of 7.5 x 6.5m. Around its south/south-eastern arc, where it was perched on a steep slope, the wall was built entirely of stone to a maximum surviving height on the inside face of almost a metre and up to five courses. This type of construction appears to have continued around the south-west arc too, although here only parts of the foundation course survived. The east and north-east section of the circuit was built differently, with large stone blocks used to face the wall inside and out but the core constructed of turves. The wall averaged 1.3m wide, so that the interior area of the hut measured 5 x 4m.

The door was almost certainly on the east, where there was a gap in the stone facing flanked on the inside by two stone blocks set upright. Between them a flat slightly worn slab appeared to be a threshold and there was a similarly worn but larger

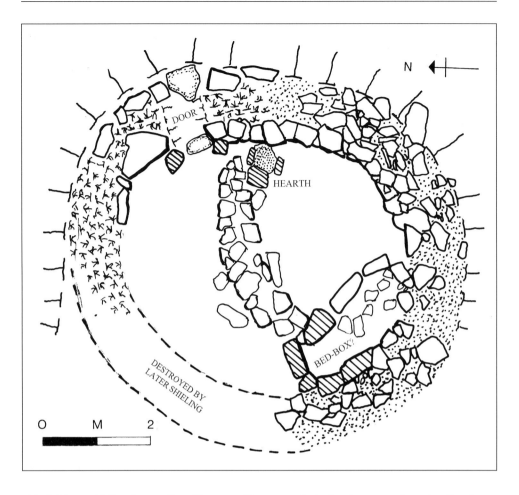

*48 A Norse shieling hut at Ben Gunnary, Barra, partly built of stone and partly of turf
with a stone facing. The name Gunarry means 'Gunnar's shieling'*

slab on the outside of the wall. The door was narrow, no more than 0.5m wide, and
could have been easily blocked to keep out the wind. The interior of the hut was
divided into two areas by a roughly laid stone foundation which ran in an arc from
the left of the door towards the rear wall. A turf superstructure could have been
erected on this foundation but we observed no signs of one. The foundation followed
the line of a low rock face, thus dividing the hut into an upper area immediately
inside the door, and a lower or sunken area (about 30cm below the upper level) in
the southern end of the hut. Within the sunken area a hearth was found tucked up
against the junction of the hut wall and the partition.

To the west of the sunken area, and 30cm above its bottom, a rectangular
structure, 2.2 x 1m, was set against the inside of the hut wall, marked out by three
large blocks set flat and by five blocks set upright at one end. We suggest this may
have been a simple box-bed the inside of which would have been filled with heather.

The sunken area was filled with a rich black peaty soil. There were no visible or clearly defined levels within this fill, but we noted that the pottery and flints found within it tended to occur in horizontal clusters. We interpret the fill and its artefact distribution as probably reflecting intermittent, perhaps seasonal use, over a period of some years.

From this deposit we recovered 31 sherds, mostly of a slightly micaceous fabric with small rounded white grits, fired from buff to grey. Two sherds in a dark grey rather laminated fabric had a grass-marked exterior face. In the same level there were also 36 pieces of flint and two of chert, of which 27 were small thin flakes. The only other find was a small steatite spindle-whorl. We date this material to the Norse period on comparison with the much larger assemblage recovered at Kilpheder on South Uist, where steatite spindle whorls, grass-marked pottery, and small thin flint flakes from fire-lighters are more abundant. So we believe this hut is a Norse shieling, and of course we would like to think it was used by a man called Gunnar!

The other structure is quite different, being a rectangular hut built with stone rubble, immediately over the Pictish period occupation in the abandoned wheel-house at Alt Chrisal. The hut was only 3.8 x 2.3m in size, and its only furnishing was an unenclosed fireplace. The small amount of pottery associated with it included no diagnostic Norse sherds, but a steatite spindle whorl identical to the one from Ben Gunnary and a handful of flint strike-a-lights, together with the structure's stratigraphic position on site, suggest it belongs in the Norse period. Again, it can have been no more than an occasional shepherd's shelter.

If there was a settlement focus for Norse occupation of Barra it should be at Borve, the only place-name which refers to a significant settlement. The name derives from Old Norse *Borg* which was a 'castle, a town'. The former is unlikely, but a substantial settlement is possible. The Borve valley and headland together provide an extensive area suitable for both pasture and cultivation. Analysis of soils and pollen buried beneath a cairn in the Borve valley confirms that in the eighth to ninth centuries AD land was being cleared of stones and used to cultivate barley. Furthermore, Borve is probably the location of the only excavated Norse burial from the island. It was found by Commander Edge in the 1860s, adjacent to a standing stone erected on a mound of sand. The only standing stone found on Barra situated on sand is that at Borve. Edge found a skeleton accompanied by two oval bronze brooches with intricate interlaced decoration, two bronze buckle tongues, a whetstone, a comb, an iron weaving sword, heckles and shears. The brooches were subsequently identified as of Scandinavian origin, manufactured in the late eighth century AD. This was clearly not the burial of a shepherd or cowherd, but rather of a Norse woman of considerable wealth and status. If she was a resident of the island rather than a visitor, then she presumably lived somewhere in the Borve valley.

Many Norse burials are associated with stone settings of some sort. Those from Cnip in Lewis had simple rectilinear arrangements of stone blocks or slabs around them, whilst examples from Orkney were inside boat-shaped settings, presumably

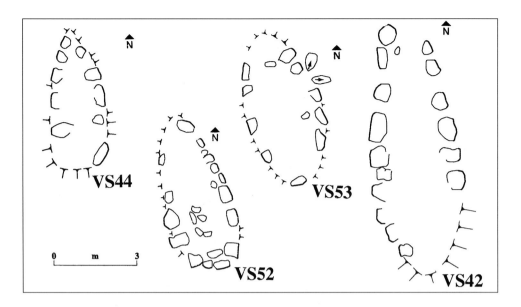

49 Four boat-shaped stone settings from Eorisdale, Vatersay. Most of the settings are too far from the coastline to be interpreted as boat noosts, but the only excavated example provided no evidence to explain their function

imitating other Viking burials made in full-size wooden boats. There are hints of the latter in nineteenth-century accounts of Viking burials on both Colonsay and Oronsay, on the other side of The Minches from Barra. We were therefore intrigued to find about 40 boat-shaped stone settings in the southern islands, and especially on Vatersay (20 examples) and Berneray (10 examples).

They vary in size from about 3-9m in length, some have a pointed prow and flat stern and others two pointed ends, and some have low mounds within them while others appear to have flat interiors (**49**). They follow no common orientation and their location varies from headlands and coastlines to hill-slopes and valleys. Excavation of an example at Eorisdale on Vatersay, where there are no less than 15 of these monuments, yielded no finds of any sort and threw no light on their function or date. The only clue to their date at all is that several on Vatersay seem to have been in existence before some of the eighteenth- and nineteenth-century land boundaries were laid out. As to their function, all we can say is that they are certainly not boat noosts – some of them are more than 200ft above sea level and hundreds of yards from the coast. Tempting as it is to see them as Norse burial places, we suspect they are not, unless they are of a purely symbolic type.

One further Norse burial on Barra remains to be mentioned however, even though the grave and any grave-goods it contained have never been found. This burial is attested by an inscribed stone slab found in 1865 in the churchyard at Kilbarr. On one side of the slab is a runic inscription which reads 'After Thorgerth, Steiner's daughter, this cross was raised'. Whether Steiner himself

50 A memorial stone with a Norse inscription on the back, recording that it was set up in memory of a woman called Thorgerth. Kilbarr, Barra. David Savory

51 *Kisimul Castle, the stronghold of Macneil of Barra, after restoration by Robert Lister Macneil, 45th chief of the Clan*

erected this slab, or it was erected by others, he was clearly a significant figure locally for him and his daughter to be commemorated in this way. The other side of the slab has an elaborate Celtic type cross carved upon it, with plaited interlace decoration (**50**). It probably dates to the late tenth or eleventh century, and clearly demonstrates that by this time some Norse in the Western Isles had been converted to Christianity.

The form of the cross on this slab is closely related to similar slightly later crosses found in the Isle of Man, which is appropriate since by the end of the eleventh century all of the Western Isles were part of the Norse kingdom of Man and the Isles. On the mainland, the Pictish and Scottish kingdoms had merged under the leadership of the Dalriadan kings, and a new political domain emerged in south-west Scotland under the dynamic leadership of Sumerled MacGillibride. He successfully challenged the kings of Man and took control of Argyll and the southern Hebrides in 1156, only to be defeated by the King of Scotland in 1164. For a while the Outer Hebrides remained under the control of the King of Norway, but following the Battle of Largs in 1263, they were ceded to the Kingdom of Scotland. Parts of the new lands were bestowed by the Scottish crown on the chiefs of various families or clans. Eventually by the mid-fourteenth century, as a result of various dynastic marriages, John of Islay came to control the whole of the Western Isles and took the title Lord of the Isles.

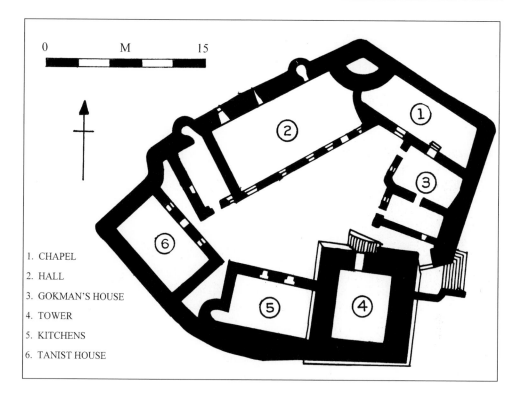

1. CHAPEL

2. HALL

3. GOKMAN'S HOUSE

4. TOWER

5. KITCHENS

6. TANIST HOUSE

52 Interior plan of Kisimul Castle, partly restored

Among the local chiefs and landholders over whom the Lord of the Isles held superiority was Macneil of Barra, who in addition to Barra and the islands south of it, also held land on Uist. In time, the Macneils erected a castle as their home and stronghold on a small rocky islet in Castlebay (**51**). Its construction took place over a long period of time, with the original curtain wall and tower being supplemented first by a chapel and hall, and then by a watchman's house and a kitchen building (**52**). A tanist house (for the heir to the chieftainship) was also built inside the fortification, but its place in the sequence is uncertain. In addition to these various additions to the accommodation provided in the original castle, there were many repairs, alterations and modifications to the fabric of the structure. The impression is of a building with a long and complex history, which, status symbol as it may have been, was also a lived-in home of the Macneil, his family and retainers.

A second status symbol was built on a small island in Loch Tangusdale, just 2.4km west of Kisimul. This was a simple three storey tower, originally 7–8m high. Its wooden-floored rooms were only about 3m square, with no fireplace and chimney, and it is difficult to believe that it was ever intended as a permanent home. Clan tradition says it was built by the chief for his half-brother Iain Garbh around 1430.

These monumental buildings are not simply the most impressive homes of the medieval period in the Barra islands, but they are the only ones – at least as far as visible remains are concerned. The houses of the chief's followers have yet to be found. Once again we must be facing a lost landscape, for the very building of Kisimul Castle and the tower in Loch Tangusdale implies that Macneil could muster a substantial labour force from amongst his kinsmen. But nowhere do we have any certain examples of their homes. To judge by recent discoveries on North Uist, we should be looking for small sub-rectangular buildings about 7-8m long externally and a little over half as wide, with stone-faced walls about 1m in width. Our survey records include perhaps half a dozen buildings which fit this description, but without excavation we are wary of ascribing them to the medieval period.

The only direct glimpses we have, therefore, of the ordinary clansmen come from the excavation of temporary summer camps or shielings. One of these overlay the earlier Norse shieling on Ben Gunnary (**53**), and was in turn covered by an early modern shieling. It comprised two elements. One was a small oval hut, with a stone-faced earth/turf wall foundation on which the superstructure was probably built of turf. Inside there were two areas of burning on its peaty floor, the larger towards the east end. A long slab set low in the outside face on the north side with no matching facing stones on the interior may have been a threshold-cum-draught-excluder.

Immediately east of this hut was a second one which appeared to butt up against it. This structure was represented by stone blocks laid flat, in places in two courses, to form two adjacent enclosed areas. Only on the east side was the stone alignment more than a single block wide, so that in most areas the blocks formed only an interior wall face. Hard packed earth outside the blocks suggested that there had probably been an earth and turf superstructure built up around the interior facing blocks. The structure comprised a totally enclosed oval space, 2 x 1.2m, at the south end, with a flat slab like a threshold forming part of its northern face. The area next to it was U-shaped, 2 x 1.4m, the open end facing north. It is possible that the builders of this structure utilised the remains of the earlier, Norse, structure to provide at least some shelter on this north side. Nowhere inside was anything resembling an occupation deposit or a hearth found, and the floor was simply the surface of the underlying silty loam into which small scraps of burnt material had been trampled. Although no pottery was found in these cabins, their stratigraphic position above a Norse hut and below an early modern one places them in the medieval period.

A very different sort of shieling shelter was excavated on a raised plateau towards the back of the Borve valley. Four low green mounds here marked the location of shielings. Excavation again revealed more than one phase of use, the lower of which produced a small assemblage of pots with thin uneven walls and flat-topped rims of medieval date. The structure they were associated with was a loose ring of stone blocks, just over 3m in diameter, with a trodden earth floor and a small hearth area on one side. It is difficult to imagine that this ring of stones was ever a built structure.

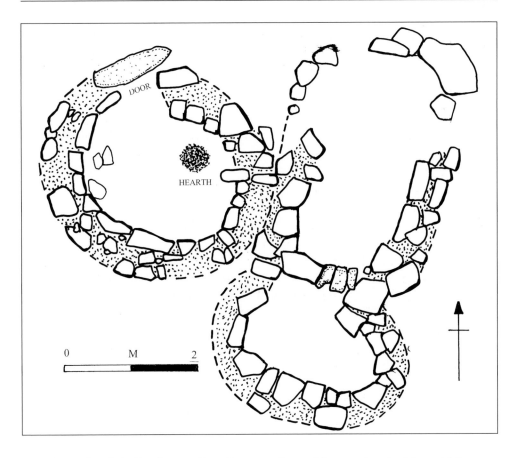

53 Two medieval shieling huts at Ben Gunnary, Barra. They overlay the Norse shieling on the same site

Rather, we believe the stones were simply brought to the site and placed around the edges of a tent-like structure to anchor it against the Hebridean winds.

We have many other shieling sites which we believe are of medieval date but without excavation it is impossible to be certain. The most convincing are a series of small sub-rectangular cabins built over the remains of an Iron Age roundhouse which in turns sits on the ruins of the chambered cairn at Balnacraig, also in the Borve valley. There are at least three superimposed phases of shieling huts here, and it is highly likely that at least the earliest of them belongs in the medieval period. A second group of shielings in Allasdale are also worthy of attention. Six prominent grassy mounds stand out in this gently sloping area of peatland (**colour plate 28**). In each case there are suggestions of a substantial building of between 8m and 10m diameter at the base of the mound, in some cases associated with a midden producing shell and small fragments of seemingly Iron Age pottery. Overlying these structures are smaller oval and sub-rectangular cabins mostly around 3-4m in length which to judge from their heavily embedded condition are

54 The north door of Kilbarr's church (from the inside); the original floor lay 2ft below ground level, but the narrowing of the door towards the top can be clearly seen

more likely medieval than modern. Other suspected medieval shielings are found on Vatersay and Mingulay.

On this evidence we might see the Norse settlement of the islands, with its apparent emphasis on cattle and sheep-raising by a relatively small resident population, merging slowly into the post-Norse medieval period, with a slowly growing population still best represented in the archaeological record by shielings. This gradual transition would not be at variance with the historical tradition, in which the Christian church provides a clear strand of continuity, interrupted only by the first century or so of Viking raids and settlement.

We have already noted the Christian symbolism of Thorgerth's stone from Kilbarr, and by the twelfth century a substantial church stood in the cemetery here (**colour plate 29**). Although it is now ruinous its main features are still visible. It was about 13m long and 5.5m wide, with the altar against the east wall. It was entered by a narrow door in the north wall (**54**), with two inward-sloping jambs which betray the influence of early medieval church architecture from Ireland. Two smaller structures flanked it to north and south (**55**). The south chapel is all but destroyed, but the north chapel has been restored and re-roofed. It was probably built as a burial aisle in the later sixteenth century, and it now houses a replica of Thorgerth's stone and some medieval or early modern grave slabs.

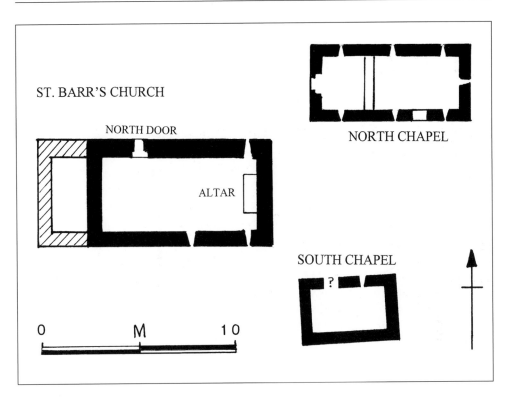

ST. BARR'S CHURCH

NORTH DOOR

NORTH CHAPEL

ALTAR

SOUTH CHAPEL

0   M   1 0

55 A restored plan of the early church and chapels at Kilbarr, Barra. The 'north chapel', which has been rebuilt and reroofed, was probably a burial aisle originally

Other medieval chapels in the islands are for the most part lost. Cille Bhride on Sandray had already disappeared in the dunes by the mid-nineteenth century, and today there is no trace of the chapel which sat atop the mounded cemetery on Pabbay. Only a short stretch of wall may survive of St Columba's chapel on Mingulay, and there is no trace of a chapel surviving alongside the mounded cemetery on Berneray. On Barra a fragment of walling and pile of collapsed stone is all that can be seen of St Brendan's chapel in the mounded corner of Borve cemetery. This leaves only Cille Bhrianain on the extreme eastern tip of north Vatersay.

Traces of this structure do survive as low humps in the grass and indicate a rather flimsy stone building about 11 x 5m with a door in the north wall. The church appears to stand in a walled enclosure measuring 25 x 20m, and material from rabbit burrows beneath its walls suggest it sits on an earlier Iron Age occupation site. Cille Bhrianain was built, according to tradition, about AD1430 by the mother of Iain Garbhe, a lady from Coll, who married Gilleonan, 29th chief of the clan Macneil. She is still recalled in Barra oral tradition as Marion of the Heads, because amongst her many sins she ordered the murder and beheading of her two step-sons. It is said that she was buried, standing upright, in Cille Bhrianain in sight of her beloved Coll, but we saw no sign of her.

The earlier chiefs of the clan Macneil were probably buried, along with other chiefs within the Lordship of the Isles, on Iona. But as the importance of Iona declined in the sixteenth century, they may have elected to be buried in the churchyard at Kilbarr. Three elaborately carved grave-slabs from the very end of the medieval period are preserved in the restored north chapel. Local tradition says they were actually brought to Kilbarr from Iona. They carry no names but both their quality and their symbolism suggest they covered the graves of Macneil's. Two feature an upright sword set in an interlaced floral design. The other, with equally elaborate interlace decoration, has a stag at its base and a galley with furled sails towards its head. The galley is one of the four emblems seen on the coat-of-arms of the Macneils.

By the end of the medieval period the Macneils had achieved a certain eminence (some might say notoriety) in the region, and tradition has it that the Macneil held himself in high regard. It is said that from the top of the tower of Kisimul Castle, his herald would declare: 'The great Macneil of Barra, having finished his meal, the princes of the earth may dine.' Roderick the Turbulent, the 35th chief, was reported to have a cellar in the castle stocked with the best French and Spanish wines, which he acquired through piracy. At this time, the chief was said to be able to muster a force of 200 fighting men, which might imply a population of between 500 and 1000 men, women and children in the Barra islands. But as we have seen, there is little recognisable trace of them in the landscape.

6 Crowded landscapes

Although the paucity of evidence for medieval occupation of the islands probably reflects the fact that they were still rather sparsely occupied, there is no doubt that it also reflects our inability to distinguish between medieval and early modern shielings, and to identify other medieval structures from survey remains alone. Indeed, we can point with confidence to no post-medieval houses before the second half of the eighteenth century, yet church records tells us that the population of the islands in 1755 stood at about 1200 souls. There is no reason to think that the population had grown rapidly in the previous two centuries, and we can reasonably assume that at the end of the medieval era the islands were inhabited by somewhere between 500 and 1000 people. It was only after 1750 that the introduction of both the potato and kelp production stimulated a population explosion.

So in what sort of houses did the seventeenth- and early eighteenth-century islanders live, before the appearance of the blackhouse, the oblong thick-walled house without chimneys, that is regarded as the archetypal Hebridean home? So far the search for the origins of the blackhouse has proved frustrating. Suggestions that early blackhouses were built in turf are interesting because such structures could provide a link to the Norse-period houses excavated by Mike Parker Pearson on South Uist. These structures, dug into the machair, are similar in size, shape, door location and interior organisation to blackhouses, and their superstructure was probably completed in turf. As they survive they give the appearance of an oblong stone-lined pit, and on the east coast of Barra we have discovered the remains of three 'blackhouses' which also have only a stone inner-wall facing, lining a slightly sunken floor area (**56**). It is tempting to think that these are examples of the blackhouse evolving, especially as the east coast of Barra is not machair so that the subterranean style of the Uist houses would soon need to be modified. But a small trial trench across the interior of one provided no evidence of an early date. The prototype turf-built blackhouse may eventually be demonstrated by excavation, but on Barra the only traces yet identified of blackhouses built entirely of turf are the remains of two houses at Rulios, known to have been erected in 1851.

An alternative prototype for the blackhouse might be structures like the small thick-walled sub-rectangular house of medieval date excavated by Ian Armit at Eilean Olabhat on North Uist. About 7.5m long and over 5m wide, it compares in size to about two dozen Barra blackhouses, and at 1.2m its walls are of similar thickness. It has a door set at one end of a long wall, and inside a simple partition, against which is set a hearth. It is probably dated to the fourteenth to fifteenth centuries. Although we

56 A blackhouse with only an inner wall face of stone, Bruernish, Barra

cannot identify any houses as early as this on Barra, in and around the settlement of Gortein facing onto the Sound of Barra, there are some similar houses which we think might be immediate predecessors of mid-eighteenth-century blackhouses.

The settlement of Gortein went into decline and was completely abandoned by about 1835. At the nucleus of the settlement there are the surviving footings of four blackhouses, which were probably amongst the first houses to be abandoned, in the 1820s. They were probably built sometime in the second half of the eighteenth century (**57**). Of interest here are not these houses, but the remains of two or three smaller, less regular buildings, which appear to underlie them. Reduced and grassed over as they are it is difficult to be certain as to their precise shape and construction, but they appear to be thick-walled structures of oblong or sub-rectangular shape, but not blackhouses as such. They apparently had gone out of use before the later eighteenth century when they were replaced by the overlying blackhouses. Stratigraphically and structurally they provide plausible forerunners of these blackhouses, and perhaps provide a glimpse of the homes of the islanders in the early modern period.

With a thousand people living in the islands by 1750, and without the valuable food resource provided by the potato plant, and the equally valuable source of cash provided by kelp production, the islanders must have relied heavily on beef, lamb, milk and cheese to supplement their barley, fish and shellfish. Many of the shelters

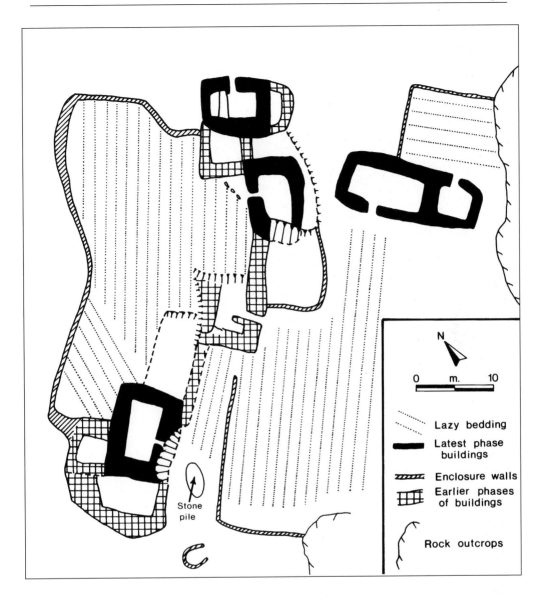

57 Plan of blackhouses at Gortein, Barra, with underlying thick-walled structures

and shielings found in the hills were probably used in this period, and by sampling several different types of shieling and shelter we have identified three examples.

The earliest also appears to be the most elaborate, and one of the most remote. It was built into the back of a small rocky knoll, about 150m above sea level near Bretadale on the south-west coast. When we found it, it was covered with heather and we could simply see that there was a stone structure, probably with more than one room. In fact, when we removed the heather and carefully cleared away top soil and debris, we found we had three separate little rooms or cabins in a row, all

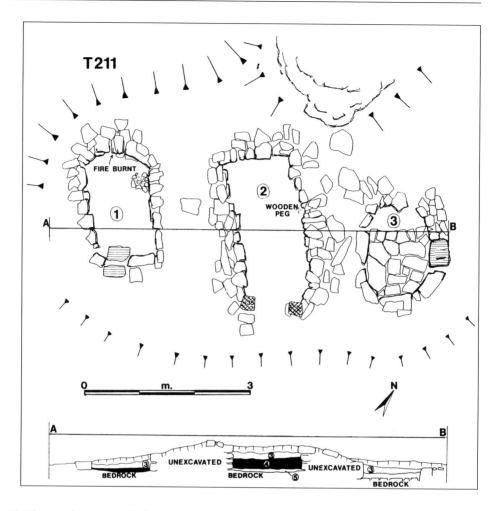

58 Three early-modern shieling cabins above Bretadale, Barra; it was probably occupied in the seventeenth century

semi–subterranean (**58**). Each cabin had its individuality, and they may each have served a separate purpose. The smallest cabin was oval, only 1.5 x 1m, with a worn threshold slab in the east side. But two-thirds of the floor was paved with slabs, and the remaining third was bare rock. Next to it was the largest cabin, a rectangular room, 2.5 x 1.2m, with a door flanked by two upright stone blocks in the south end. It was the best preserved room, with walls standing 0.5m high, but it was empty apart from a pointed wooden peg with a perforated head, found on the earth floor against the foot of the wall. The westernmost cabin was 2 x 1m with two worn slabs in the south-facing door, an earth floor and a small fireplace in the far corner. The wooden peg was C14 dated to *c*.1520-1670, but no other artefacts of any kind were found. This emphasises that these small cabins were used for temporary shelter rather than any sort of prolonged occupation, but as shelters go

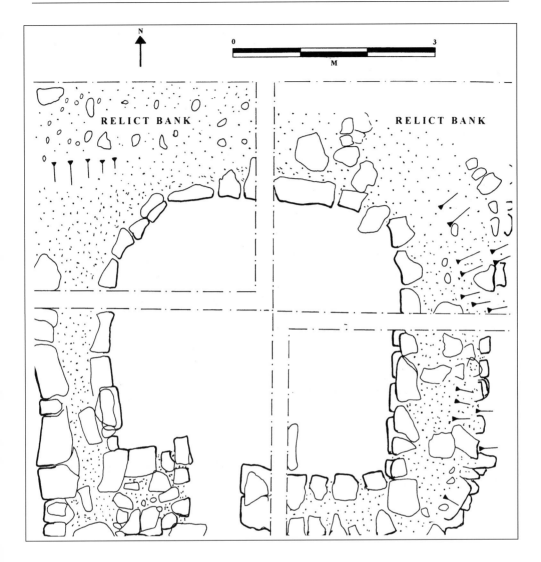

59 An eighteenth-century D-shaped shieling hut, Borve valley

this was a relatively sophisticated structure. It is tempting to see the rooms as providing an east-to-west 'suite' of store-room, bedroom, and living room. But both local tradition and the frequent appearance of shelters and shieling huts in pairs would support the alternative interpretation that the two larger cabins were used to segregate the young men and women who used the summer shielings.

A more substantial but simpler hut was found at about 170m over sea level, above the Borve valley on Barra. This was a square building erected against a boundary bank, with walls about 1m thick, a door in the middle of the south wall, and a single room 3.5m square (**59**). It had an earth floor, but no obvious hearth area. The only clue to its date was a fragment of later seventeenth-century glazed pottery trodden

121

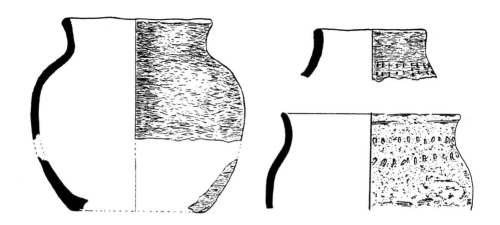

60 Handmade early modern pottery from Borve (lower right) and Allasdale

into the floor. It was abandoned, probably not long after it was built, but it was later rebuilt with a curving rear wall. Only a single sherd of early eighteenth-century pottery was found on the earth floor. Although this hut provided much more space and was more solidly built than the one above Bretadale, it too was clearly only used for short periods of time, probably during the summer.

Only 200m west of this hut, on a rather exposed plateau, a group of four or five low green mounds with stone blocks poking through the turf have all the marks of temporary summer shelters. Excavation of one revealed two phases of use, the earlier in the medieval period. The secondary use of the site was marked by the remains of a probably sub-rectangular and simply built structure which had almost certainly been robbed of much of its stone for building later walls or huts nearby. It was more ephemeral than either of the other sites, and may have been little more than a stone wind-break around a tent-like structure. In contrast to the glazed sherds from the D-shaped hut nearby, this shelter yielded a substantial piece from a storage jar of handmade, unglazed pottery decorated with stab marks around its shoulder, looking more like prehistoric than modern pottery (**60**). But vessels of this sort are known from elsewhere in the Hebrides and date to the seventeenth to eighteenth century AD.

This last site is typical of hundreds of simple structures found in the higher, rough pastures all over Barra and its neighbouring islands. Many of the smallest are little more than rings of stone which may have been used to peg down a blanket over a shepherd. Others were perhaps windbreaks built around tents made of blankets or skins, and others were a little more substantial and had a low built wall within which a shepherd could take shelter overnight. We have excavated two examples of this type of shelter, each providing less than 2m² of space, but as expected, they yielded no material evidence of their occupiers at all. They are important, however, as the most widespread testimony we have to the continuous and extensive use of the rough pasture on these bare, wind-swept hills by successive generations of island families.

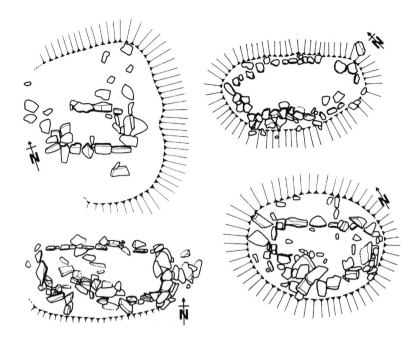

61 Some of the 120 peat-drying platforms found on the high ground of Mingulay

Visiting the islands today one sees only sheep on the hill-pastures; cattle are confined to the machair of Eoligarry, Greian, and Borve on Barra, and to Traigh Varlish and southern Vatersay. But early visitors to Barra mention the small black cattle as being an important part of the livestock. Walker reported that in the 1760s Barra was exporting about 140 head of black cattle a year, in addition to casks of salted beef. According to MacQueen, by 1794 the number of cattle exported annually had risen to 200-250; there were over 1000 cattle on the island, and twice as many sheep. Oral tradition certainly associates the use of the sheilings with the seasonal movement of the cattle to the upland pastures.

Not all of the shelters, however, are necessarily associated with the activities of shepherds and cowherds. The hill-slopes of the islands were also important sources of peat, the only fuel locally available in quantity, and the hillsides are scarred with old peat cuttings. Amongst the peat cuttings are the remains of simple shelters and huts which offered refuge from the rainstorms which sweep across the islands even in the peat-cutting and drying months from May to August. Nowhere is the importance of peat more clearly demonstrated than on Mingulay, where the summits of Carnan and Tom a Mhaide are covered with low oval and sub-rectangular stone-edged mounds and platforms that were probably used as bases on which to stack drying peat from the surrounding peatfields (**61**). Altogether about 120 of these platforms have been identified, and nearly as many shelters, scattered between them. The intensity of peat extraction on Mingulay is perhaps partly explained by the absence of peatfields on nearby Berneray, whose inhabitants had to ship it across from their larger neighbour.

It is also on Mingulay that we have the best-preserved field systems dating back before the Crofting Commission of the late nineteenth century. The fact that Mingulay was totally abandoned by 1912 means that the older field boundaries have suffered much less from modification and destruction than those of Barra and Vatersay. Around the south-eastern quarter of the island is a network of field banks and walls which consists of relatively large enclosed fields flanked at the north and west ends by irregular complexes of smaller fields and enclosures. That at the north is immediately alongside the settlement occupied until 1912, and the area south of the village stream is divided by a series of regular, straight croft boundaries. North of the stream there are no such boundaries, however, and an apparently older system of small irregular fields and plots or enclosures survives.

At the south-western corner of the entire network another archaic looking group of irregular enclosures is found in Skipisdale, which seems to have had no permanent houses contemporary with the settlement in the bay (**62**). Within the Skipisdale complex there are remains of buildings which appear to belong with the enclosures. Site 345 close to the north-west corner of the complex seems to incorporate the remains of a large prehistoric roundhouse over which are built a dozen or more small sub-circular cabins built in four or five clusters. Downslope and on the other side of the stream is a second less well-defined cluster of cabins (site 346), which also appear to be overlying the remains of a second prehistoric house. Two further structures, an oblong building 5 x 3.5m (site 348), and another 5 x 2m (site 350), are outside the main enclosure wall. House 348 at least is later than this enclosure wall, being butted up against it. How old the Skipisdale enclosure complex and the cabins within it are is uncertain. Dodgshon has argued that complexes of irregular fields like these are incompatible with the runrig system of land use and may pre-date its development. In that case they might be of later medieval date or perhaps belong, in these southern islands, to the early modern period.

On Barra, one area of the Borve valley appears to preserve traces of a similar complex of enclosures. Between the rocky slopes of Beinn Mhartainn and Grianan in Craigston township, an area of hillside has been extensively cleared. It is enclosed by a substantial earth and stone bank, and divided into a series of fields of irregular size and shape (**63**). Though better preserved up-slope, they appear to have extended down to the stream in the floor of the valley. There are some surviving traces of similar enclosed fields on the other side of the stream too. There are no clusters of cabins inside these enclosures, however, but only two blackhouses towards the east side of the complex. Further blackhouses are found outside the enclosed system, to the west. Later croft boundaries certainly ignore all but the main enclosing bank, and again we can be certain that the irregular enclosures are part of a pre-crofting field system, but possibly no earlier than eighteenth-century in date.

If irregular field enclosures were still being constructed in the eighteenth century, then it is difficult to see the context in which the runrig system of agri-culture was practised in the islands. Runrig was the method of organising arable land, whereby each tenant's holding was a dispersed series of rigs, spread amongst the similar dispersed holdings of the other tenants in the township. It would be

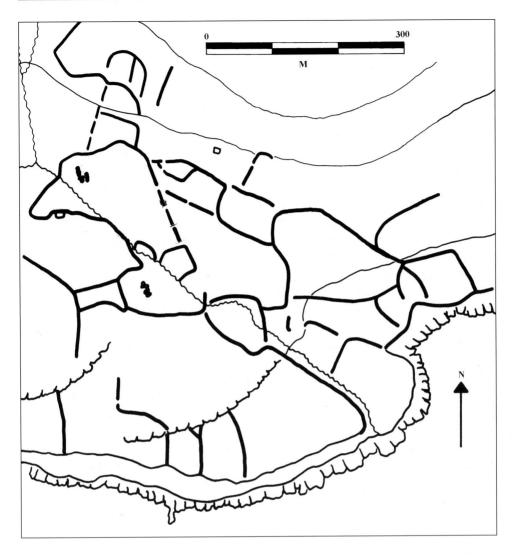

62 A pre-crofting field system at Skipisdale, Mingulay, with hut complexes and two oblong buildings

simplest to assume that runrig was never adopted in the Barra islands. But a 40-year-old crofter who gave evidence to the Crofting Commission in 1883 says that runrig was in operation during the time of his grandfather, which we must assume was in the early nineteenth century. It may be that runrig came late to Barra, perhaps during the eighteenth century, and that the enclosures at Borve pre-date the introduction of runrig.

Be that as it may, within these enclosures there are clear traces of arable cultivation in the form of narrow rig, and on some steep slopes particularly narrow but high rigs which are relict lazy-beds. There are also many scattered clearance cairns, mostly

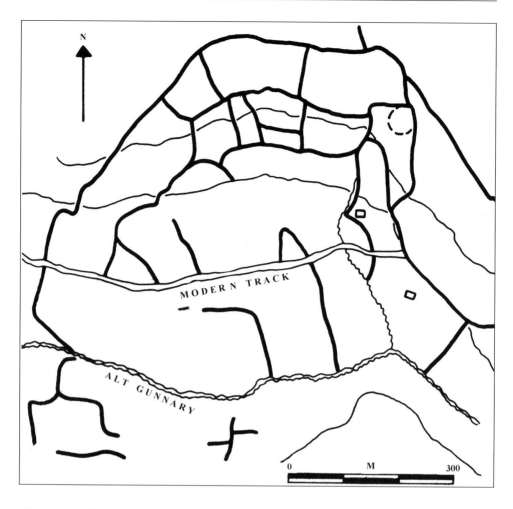

63 A pre-crofting field system, Craigston, Borve valley, Barra

of small field stones, suggesting they represent secondary rather than primary clearance. Larger stones and rocks moved in the first stages of clearance for agriculture were probably used to build the walls and earth-and-stone banks of the enclosures. Lazy-beds, narrow rig and clearance cairns are to be found over extensive areas of Barra and Vatersay and in more limited areas on the smaller islands (**colour plate 30**). They attest, again, to a rapidly growing population in the eighteenth and nineteenth centuries. Some of the narrow rig was almost certainly produced by pony-drawn ploughs, which according to John Macculloch, who visited Barra in 1816, was the 'ristle plough; an ancient instrument carrying the coulter alone, and preceding that which contains the share'. But much of it may have been the product of laborious digging with the spade. John Walker who visited Barra in 1764 said that 'a great part' of the cultivated land 'was manufactured with the spade', which was better suited to the very small plots of land of many tenants. Dodgshon has suggested that spade-cultivation was particularly common in times of population pressure in areas with limited areas of arable land. This is certainly a fair description of Barra in the period *c.*1770-1850. Barley was still the principal crop grown on arable land in Barra and its islands, just as it had been 5000 years before. This is confirmed by the Reverend MacQueen in his report on Barra in 1794. Oats, which had become an important crop elsewhere in the Highlands and Islands, was grown only in small quantities, and in 1840, barley-meal was still one half of the staple diet.

The other half of course was the potato, which had been introduced into the Western Isles in the 1750s. John Walker is quite explicit about the introduction of the potato to Barra, which he says took place 12 years before his visit, that is in 1752. The potato rapidly became not simply a significant part of the island diet but by far the most important food source the islanders had. It could be grown on lazy-beds dug even on the steepest of slopes, and in the smallest plots of land between rocky outcrops. It produced a higher yield than oats or barley, required relatively little looking after, and could be easily stored for long periods. The intensity of its culti-vation is witnessed by hundreds of relict lazy-bed plots in and around settlement areas throughout the islands.

The lazy-beds, and the narrow rig, were manured with seaweed which was carted by ponies from the rocky coasts of the islands. Early visitors comment how important the use of seaweed fertiliser was to the successful growing of potato, oats and barley. But as early as 1794, the Rev. MacQueen says that the crofters were being prevented from taking the seaweed to fertilise their fields and plots because the landlord (Macneil of Barra) was getting such a good price for kelp. Kelp was the product of seaweed that had been burnt to reduce it to a thick liquid which cooled and hardened into a brittle variegated substance rich in alkali. This was used in the manufacture of soap, alum and glass. Its manufacture began on a significant scale in the Hebrides about 1750. When the Napoleonic Wars began and the usual source of alkali, Spanish barilla, was no longer available the price of Hebridean kelp climbed steeply. In 1794 it was £4-5 a ton, by 1797 it was fetching nearer £9, and when Napoleon met Wellington at Waterloo in 1815 it was £10-11 a ton.

MacQueen says in 1794 that Barra was exporting about 200 tons of kelp to Leith and Liverpool. Since more than 20 tons of seaweed was needed to produce a ton of kelp, this means that the crofters were cutting and processing about 4000 tons of seaweed a year. John Macculloch in 1816 says that the crofters spent three months in the summer collecting seaweed and reducing it to kelp, and further that undertaking this work was a condition of their tenancy. It was clearly a major enterprise, and source of income, to both crofter and landlord, but it has left remarkably little trace in the landscape. Around the coasts of Barra we have found perhaps 20 small kelp ovens — long, narrow pits lined with stones around their sides. With one notable exception which we shall examine in more detail in our final chapter, these are the only surviving traces of this important industry.

Its real significance was not however the wealth it brought to the landlord, but rather its effects on both agriculture and demography. Because so much of the short Hebridean summer had to be devoted to producing kelp, the crofters had little time

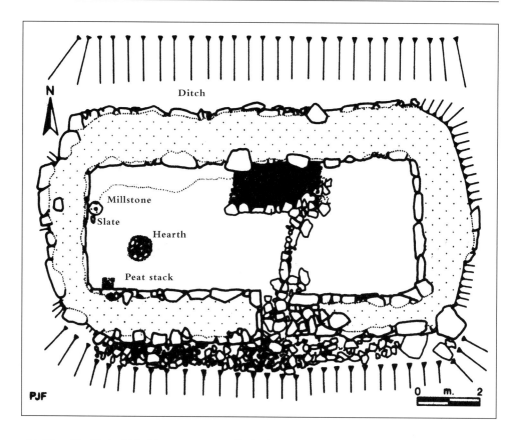

64 The Alt Chrisal blackhouse as originally built in the late eighteenth century

to attend to their crops. So they became increasingly reliant on the potato which needed relatively little attention while it was growing, was quick to harvest, and could be eaten or stored with a minimum of preparation. At the same time, the income which the crofters earned from making kelp – between £2 and £2-10/- a ton – meant that they were less dependent on cattle and crops to pay their rent. The coincidence of the introduction of the potato and kelp production in the 1750s created a situation in which the islands were able to support a population not only larger than ever before, but also beyond the agricultural carrying capacity of the land. At the same time it was in the landlord's interests to encourage this population explosion which enabled him to produce more kelp and collect more rent.

The parish of Barra's population doubled between 1750 and 1840 from about 1200 to 2400 people. Of these, in the census of 1841, 113 lived on Mingulay, 84 on Vatersay, about 20 on each of Berneray and Pabbay, and a dozen on Sandray. The rest were to be found in the townships of Barra itself. This burgeoning population is represented today by the decaying but still visible remains of 200 black-houses, mostly on Barra but found on all the other islands too, including offshore islands like Fuiay. There is even a single blackhouse on the grim and bleak 200 acres of rock known as Muldoanich. All of these houses shared the same basic features (**64**). They were thick-walled oblong buildings with rounded external corners, and walls built of unmortared stone facing and an earth core. There was a single door, usually more or less central in one of the long walls. The walls probably never stood much above a metre in height, and had at best one or two tiny windows set where the wall met the steeply pitched roof, the supports for which were placed on the inside edge of the walls rather than the outside. The roof was covered with straw, reeds or turf, and there were no fireplaces set into the walls, and no chimneys. Smoke from the hearth escaped through a hole in roof, after circulating around the rafters and blackening ceiling and walls. Hence, together with the near-absence of daylight, the term 'blackhouse'.

Blackhouses are found throughout the highlands and islands and because they all employ similar materials and construction techniques, they are often thought to be of uniform design throughout the entire region. In discovering and recording the structural remains of 200 houses, however, we have noticed that in several respects the blackhouses of Barra and its islands differ from the 'archetypal' blackhouse as seen at Arnal in Lewis and Sollas in North Uist. They differ even from the houses on the neighbouring island of South Uist.

It is axiomatic that blackhouses provided accommodation for people and animals under the same roof, and indeed in the same room. The report of the Royal Commission on the Housing of the Working Class published in 1885 described the blackhouse thus: 'there is no partition between the byre, the kitchen and the sleeping apartment: in which all the inhabitants, human and bestial, live under the same roof in the same open space'. Joseph Mitchell in 1883 said that houses were 'from 30 to 60ft long; the greater part appropriated by the cattle, and the family separated occasionally by a mere turf partition'. A sample of blackhouses surveyed by colleagues on South Uist confirmed that they ranged from 10–30m in length, and that the majority provided over 40m^2 of internal floor space. Living space for the family, as opposed to the animals, is variously estimated between 15m^2 and 25m^2.

Over half of the Barra blackhouses are less than 10m long, and only one in eight provided as much as 40m^2 of total floor space. That is, the Barra blackhouses are much shorter and smaller in area than their relations to the north. In general terms, the total floor area they provided was comparable to that given over only to human occupation in the blackhouses of the Uists and Lewis and Harris. There are other structural differences too. Almost half of the Uist blackhouses have two opposed doors, one in each long wall, a feature found in just a single example on Barra. The majority of Barra blackhouses have their single door more or less central in the front wall, whereas the blackhouses on the islands to the north tend to have the door towards one end of the building.

These differences clearly suggest not only that the Barra blackhouses provided less space than the archetypal blackhouse, but that this space was used in a different way. The fact is that there was simply not enough room in the majority of Barra blackhouses for both people and animals. This is all the more so because the population of the Barra islands was 90 per cent Catholic and likely therefore to have larger

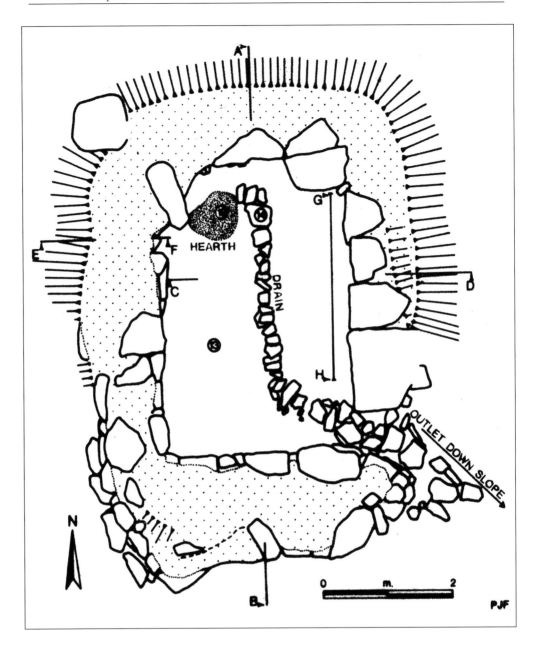

65 The byre adjacent to the Alt Chrisal blackhouse. The door is typically in one corner, through which runs a drain

families than the Protestant islanders further north. The Rev. Nicholson in 1840 recorded the parish's population as 2097 and the number of families as 371, suggesting an *average* household of five to six persons. Many households would have been larger than the average of course, and families of eight or nine were not uncommon. We are quite certain, therefore, that the vast majority of Barra black-houses could provide room only for the crofter and his family.

This has been confirmed by our excavation of five blackhouses on Barra. In every case there was no evidence for a cobbled surface and drain at one end as part of the provision needed for overwintering animals. Further, many Barra blackhouses have separate byres. In some cases they are attached to one end of the blackhouse but have their own entrance and there is no direct access from living area to byre. More often there is a free-standing byre built nearby. We excavated one of these alongside the blackhouse at Alt Chrisal (**65**). It was built in the same manner, but more crudely, than the blackhouse and had a door in one corner. A simple, roughly covered drain ran down the middle of the building and exited through the door. Final confirmation that the majority of the people of the Barra isles rejected the idea of stalling animals in the same room as that in which they lived is provided by an article in the *Inverness Courier* published in December 1845, written by 'a late resident'. This says that the people of Barra 'are considerably in advance of their more northerly neighbours, as they have outhouses for their cattle and horses, though these may still be seen in one end of their dwelling-house in a very few instances'. The few exceptions are probably to be found amongst the largest of the Barra blackhouses, often with traces of internal partitions, and located on the west coast and at Vaslain, where the best and largest areas of cattle pasture are to be found.

So if the animals were banned from the Barra blackhouse, how was the living area used? The first point to make, already touched on above, is that the Barra families were large. A study of 70 migrant families to Canada reveals that they averaged around eight individuals and that one in four families consisted of ten or more people. Few houses would have offered as much as 5m² of space per family member, and many provided less than 3m². The norm for peasant families around the world is around 10m², so by any standards the Barra blackhouse was a crowded home.

It was also in many respects a very spartan environment. The thick walls kept out the persistent winds which sweep the islands and by thickening the walls as they approached the doorway, a deep 'porch' was created to protect the living room from gusts. But inside the walls were of rough, unworked stone with no plaster or cladding, unmortared and with gaps between the stones filled with moss and heather. The floor was of beaten or trampled earth and contemporary descriptions carry no reference to rugs or carpets.

Barra was notorious for having no supplies of wood other than what driftwood could be collected from the shore. There was thus little furniture inside the black-houses and in excavating five blackhouses we have found no clear evidence for the existence of bed-boxes of the kind seen in the preserved blackhouses further north in the island chain. It is quite likely that the people of the Barra isles continued to sleep, as Buchanan had reported in 1782, 'upon the ground, strewing ferns or heather on the floor'. Common sense suggests that sleeping areas would be in the darker recesses of the room, away from the door and its drafts.

It is for this reason that we believe a small cobbled area framed with larger stones, set against the rear wall opposite the front door in James Campbell's blackhouse at

66 A hard-standing, facing the front door, probably for a dresser; the Alt Chrisal blackhouse

Alt Chrisal, was not the base for a bedbox, but a stand for a simple dresser (**66**). Given the scarcity of wood the dresser may have been no more than two or three planks recovered from the shore, supported on blocks of stone. In itself it would have been a source of some pride, and decorated with the best of the family's crockery it would have been a statement of their comparative wealth. A similar stand, too narrow ever to have taken a bed-box was found – again opposite the front door – in a blackhouse at Balnabodach.

The broken crockery found in the blackhouses we have excavated is particularly interesting as it reflects both the diet and the overseas connections of the crofters. Large stoneware jars seem to have been used for storage, but the bulk of the pottery at both Alt Chrisal and Balnabodach was from bowls of various sorts, which probably reflects the prevalence of broths, stews and porridge in the diet. Teapots and cups confirm that tea was a popular beverage by the mid-eighteenth century, although there are also plenty of bottle fragments to support the observation of several early visitors that the Barra men enjoyed their whiskey. The bulk of the crockery came from the Scottish potteries and the cheap and colourful spongeware was particularly popular (**colour plate 31**). But pottery was also acquired from Liverpool and Stoke, and from Tyneside, most probably from pedlars working their way through the island chain. Later in the nineteenth century, some of the pottery from the east coast Scottish and English potteries was probably brought back by fishermen who followed the herring around the north coasts of Britain each summer. For people who were amongst the poorest in the British Isles, the acquisition of colourful crockery must have had a social significance which is hard for us to appreciate today.

Other purchases from the outside world were few, but clay tobacco pipes have been found in all the excavated blackhouses to date and again confirm the words of a contemporary report that the men of the Barra islands were 'addicted to tobacco'.

A few articles of clothing were apparently obtained from the mainland, including shoes, printed fabrics, and the white cotton 'napkins' worn as a head covering by the women. Some woollen cloth was also brought in from the mainland for making jackets, trousers and capes. But much of the woollen material was made on the island, and in 1840 much wool was still spun on the distaff rather than the wheel.

Once the wool was spun and woven, then it was waulked, a process involving the raising and pressing of the fabric against a fluted board, which produced a thicker, firmer texture. The importance of waulking was as much social as technical, however, for it involved a whole group of women who would come to the black-house of the cloth's producer and take part in the process. While the processing continued, traditional waulking songs were sung to help with the rhythm of the work, and once the job was finished, a communal meal would follow, around the household hearth.

The hearth was the social focus of the house, and in the Barra blackhouses it was most commonly found (at least in the houses excavated by us), towards one end of the room, well away from the door. At Alt Chrisal the hearth was circular and its base was made of small cobbles pressed into the floor. In the largest of the houses at Balnabodach it was square, made of stone blocks and a few bricks probably brought to the island as ballast in a ship. It was around these hearths, especially on the long windy nights of the Hebridean winter, that traditional tales would be told and the family's history handed down from one generation to another.

Because blackhouses are associated with crofting it is tempting to think of them each standing in splendid isolation within the boundaries of its own croft. But the earliest blackhouses certainly pre-date the introduction of the croft. It was only around 1800 that multi-tenant farms and their field systems began to be replaced by small, individual holdings or crofts, often deliberately located so as to use as little decent arable land as possible and force the tenant to engage in kelping and fishing. Before the laying out of the crofts, many tenants lived in a nucleated settlement. We have already seen one of these at Gortein, and noted that its origins must go back at least into the earlier eighteenth century and possibly earlier. A cluster of nine thick-walled buildings in Allasdale includes at least four blackhouses as well as two outbuildings, and like Gortein there are traces of earlier oblong buildings obliterated or partly overlain by the latest blackhouses.

Another example is found at Crubisdale, a settlement which like Gortein was progressively abandoned between about 1820 and 1835 (**67**). Crubisdale is tucked into a fold in the rocky slopes on the east side of the Tangaval peninsula. Here six blackhouses are laid out in line, sheltering below an east-facing scarp, on a slightly raised natural platform fronted by a stream. There are enclosed areas of lazy-bedding

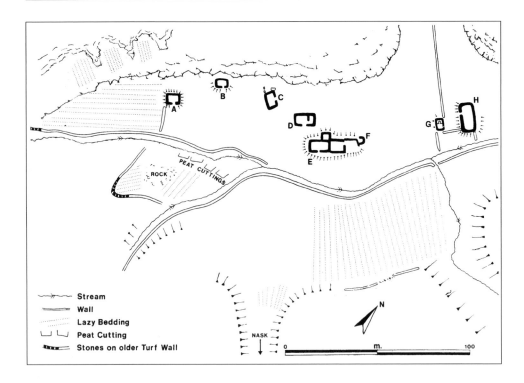

67 Plan of the blackhouse settlement at Crubisdale, where local tradition records that boat-building was practised

on both sides of the stream, and three small isolated patches on a shelf near the top of the scarp. These are each so small they can only have been used for potatoes, and the same may apply to the small enclosed cultivation plot where the stream is joined by a tributary. There were also peat cuttings here, though not enough to have supplied the inhabitants for very long. The remaining cultivated areas, including the largest one across the stream, were probably used for growing barley. We can be certain that barley was grown by the people of Crubisdale, because the largest black-house at the north end of the settlement has a drying shed with a raised floor and flue at one end. Several short banks built around this house create an enclosure by the stream, presumably used for livestock. The main enclosure walls around the culti-vated plots are the type designed to keep sheep out, with a vertical stone face on one side and a sloping earth bank on the other, and sheep no doubt formed an important part of the settlement's economy because most of the land around Crubisdale is suited only to rough pasture.

One, unusual, aspect of Crubisdale's life and times, however, may not be easily recognised from its surface remains. There is a persistent oral tradition that boats were built here. At first sight this seems unlikely, for Crubisdale is about 70m above sea level and 600m from the nearest shore. But there is a natural 'slipway' (a shallow dyke) which runs from Crubisdale to the sea at Nask, and Calum Macneil of Nask recalls often picking up iron clinker nails at Crubisdale as a boy. It may be that involvement in boat building explains the unusual structure of blackhouse E, which in addition to a lean-to against the rear wall, has a shed almost 7m square, entered from a partly enclosed yard area built onto the north end of the house. These structures do not look like the byres and barns found adjacent to other blackhouses, and they may have been used for boat-building. John Macculloch, who visited the island in 1816, noted that the Barra boats were 'very peculiar' and were built on the island, of timber purchased from northern traders.

Boats played an increasingly important part in the economy of the islands as the population outgrew the ability of the land to support it. Fish and shellfish had always contributed to the diet of the islanders, but the archaeological evidence suggests that the vast majority of fish consumed by early populations were caught either from onshore or close in-shore.

Early visitors to the islands – Dean Munro in 1549, Walter MacFarland in 1620, and Martin Martin in 1665 – all comment on the abundance of cod and ling off the east coast of Barra. The same is noted by John Walker in 1764, but he adds that the islanders do little to exploit this resource and blames it on 'the smallness and insufficiency of their boats', which denied them access to the best fishing bank six miles off the coast.

By 1794, when the Reverend MacQueen wrote the Statistical Account, 20-30 small boats were said to spend the months of April to June catching cod and ling off the east coast, and he records that in 1787 some 30,000 ling were sent to Glasgow by the Barra fishermen.

Fishing was clearly on the increase, a development almost certainly related to the increase in human population and the need to find new sources of food and income. Between 1760 and 1790, the population of the parish had risen by 30 per cent. It rose even more dramatically over the next 30 years to reach 2300 by 1820, and if we are to believe John Macculloch, significant developments in local fishing accompanied this increase. Now, in 1816, Macculloch can describe the Barra men as 'amongst the most active and industrious fishermen in Scotland'. Their boats are no longer small, manned by a crew of five, and poorly equipped with tackle. Now 'they are of considerable size, so as easily to carry ten or twelve men . . . they are swift and safe', and this presumably means they were now able to exploit the further fishing bank with some confidence if not with impunity.

Archaeologically this development in fishing activity is reflected not so much by the appearance of boat noosts, simple jetties, and fishermen's bothies or shelters, although all of these are found on the islands' coasts, but rather by a growing concentration of blackhouses on the east coast and the small islands just offshore. The coast line of Bruernish on Barra has the densest distribution anywhere in the island group. Clusters of blackhouses on islands like Gighay and Fuiay must have been occupied by people who relied heavily on the sea for their livelihood. The families occupying the eight blackhouses at Rubh an Anseig on Fuiay (**68**) could not have been supported by the 200 acres of rugged, steep-sided rough pasture which is all the island offers for farming.

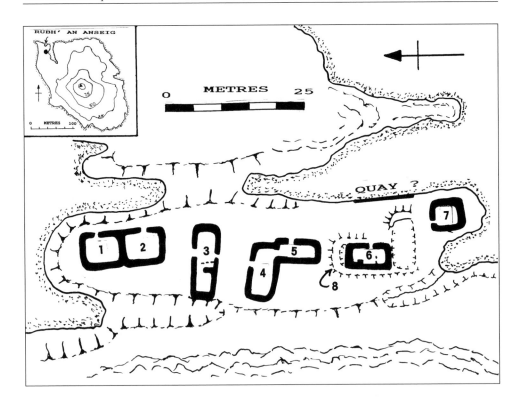

68 Survey plan of the fishing village on the isle of Fuiay

In fact, Fuiay may be seen as a microcosm for the whole island group by the time that Barra acquired a new landlord in 1840. All the southern islands, except Mingulay, were at their population peak, there were close to 2000 people living on Barra itself, and islands like Fuiay, Gighay, Hellisay, and even tiny Flodday, were occupied. These crowded landscapes were simply incapable of supporting such populations on the produce of farming alone. They had been able to sustain these growing numbers due to the income generated by kelp production, the increasing exploitation of the fisheries, and above all the god-send of the potato. Just as an island like Fuiay was over-populated, so were dozens of crofts. Colonel Macneil had allowed his tenants to take in relatives to share their crofts, not least because it provided extra hands for kelping. These small plots of just two or three acres were now often peopled by two or even three families, only one of whom paid rent. The others were known as cottars. By 1840, over half of the people occupying land in Barra were cottars. All over the island, one comes across examples of two apparently contemporary blackhouses within a few metres of each other; occasionally a croft is occupied by three blackhouses. In most cases these are the homes of tenants and cottars, perhaps 12-20 people, all dependent for their livelihood on the potatoes they could grow on their small plot of poor quality ground, the fish they could catch in the sea, and the market for kelp. If any one of these sources of support failed, intense hardship was unavoidable; if two failed, disaster was inevitable.

7 Foreign landscapes

Colonel Roderick Macneil, 40th chief of the Clan Macneil and owner of Barra and the southern islands, died in 1822 to be succeeded by his son, Roderick, at that time also a Colonel, but usually known by his later rank as General Macneil. The General inherited debts of at least £30,000 from his father, and as we have seen in the previous chapter he also inherited a much over-populated estate. The situation was exacerbated by the effects of the defeat of Napoleon in 1815. This had reduced the opportunities for military service and its financial rewards, and also allowed Spanish barilla to once more compete with kelp as a source of alkali to glass and soap manufacturers in Britain. The General thus found himself in a very difficult position, with a burgeoning population, unable to feed itself and pay its rents, and with creditors pressing for their money.

The General developed a three-part strategy to try and turn the estate's affairs around. He decided to move crofters from the best machair pastures in the north and west of the island to the east and south coasts. The released lands would then be rented out as farms to cattlemen from the mainland, and the displaced crofters would earn a living mainly by a mixture of fishing and kelping. A new fishing village would be built on the south coast of the island, in Castlebay, and deep-sea fishermen from Caithness would be brought to Barra to teach the local men how to exploit the richer fishing grounds beyond the inshore banks. Finally, a chemical factory would be built to re-process kelp and produce a high-grade source of alkali that could successfully compete with imported barilla and be sold at a much higher price than ordinary kelp.

Some of this activity can be traced in the archaeological record. We noted in the previous chapter the concentration of blackhouses found on the east coast of Barra and particularly around Bruernish. Many of the blackhouses here are perched on the seashore, surrounded by boggy peatlands, and with only tiny patches of cultivable land nearby (**69**). Although these houses are unexcavated, and therefore undated, its seems likely that most of them reflect the General's redistribution of the population. All traces of the fishing village at Castlebay have long since disappeared under the thriving present-day settlement. But the remains of the chemical factory survive at Northbay and they suggest that this was a serious, if flawed, attempt to revive the ailing kelp industry.

Although much of the factory was demolished in the 1870s, the enclosure wall survives and reveals an establishment measuring about 50m square. On the seaward side, the wall was pierced by no less than eight large entrance ports, which gave way immediately onto the waters of Northbay (**colour plate 32**). The thresholds stand

69 A blackhouse on the edge of the sea, Bruernish. Rough pasture, peat and the sea were the only resources available to the family that lived here

just above the high-tide mark, and suggest that heavily laden boats were able to approach the factory and unload their cargoes, of made-kelp from Uist, and perhaps peat fuel from the east side of Bruernish, directly into it. There are also projecting stone-built jetties at either end of the seaward wall. Inside the factory, little remains of the original structure, but there appears to have been three successive levels of flooring rising from the seaward side to the rear of the factory. At the west end of the second terrace was some sort of boiler or furnace house with a tall brick chimney. Not only is it impossible to deduce from the surviving remains what processes were applied in the factory, but it is clear from the surviving correspondence of some of Macneil's creditors that even at the time the process was shrouded in mystery.

Building such a large factory, and purchasing made-kelp from the neighbouring Uists to re-process, required considerable investment. Some of this came from the General himself, who took out further loans to finance the project, and some came from a Liverpool manufacturer. By 1836, some of Macneil's creditors were prepared to wait no longer for their money and he was declared bankrupt when he could not meet a demand for payment. Trustees took over the running of the estate and in 1838 it was put up for auction. However, all three top bidders failed to lodge a deposit against the purchase and the estate continued to be run by the trustees, until December 1840 when it was eventually bought by Colonel Gordon of Cluny.

Gordon of Cluny was a rich man who had already purchased other estates in the highlands and islands with an eye to turning them into profit-making businesses. He had a bad reputation as a landlord, and there is no doubt that initially he regarded his new tenants as simply a source of rent revenue. For this reason he appears to have rejected advice that he should send at least half of the population of Barra off to north America, and he invested a certain amount of money in 'improvements', mostly to improve the roads and trackways on the island. But his tenants were finding it difficult to pay their rents because there was no longer cash to be earned from kelping, and they were now heavily dependent on their potato crop for their subsistence.

In 1845 potato blight broke out in Britain and Ireland with devastating consequences, but by luck the Western Isles largely avoided the disease, and even exported potatoes at good prices at the beginning of 1846. Later that year, however, the luck ran out and the island chain was hit by an almost complete failure of that year's potato crop. The people of Barra and the southern isles were reduced to near starvation, surviving only by eating the seed-grain set aside for the following year. Gordon did nothing to help and it was left to the government and charitable institutions to send limited amounts of relief. But the blight persisted, and not just into 1847 but, with varying degrees of severity, for the next decade. Gordon did eventually send food supplies to his tenants, though they were expected to undertake work on his 'improvements' in exchange for it.

As the potato famine continued, however, and outside relief declined, Gordon followed the example of other landlords in the highlands and islands, and decided to 'clear' a substantial part of Barra's population. In 1850 and 1851, between 800 and 1000 people were cleared from the parish. Some were sent to Tobermory and from there dispersed to Glasgow, Edinburgh and other parts of the lowlands. Those who were removed in 1851 were sent to board the ship *Admiral* at Loch Boisdale (South Uist) in August, and from there sailed directly across the Atlantic and were deposited at Quebec. Gordon paid their passage, but otherwise they were given nothing and had little left of their own to take with them. They arrived in Canada utterly destitute, and after receiving relief from the Canadian authorities were sent on westwards. Some at least were settled around London and Williams in Ontario.

With a third of the population 'cleared', the landscape of Barra in 1851 must have been littered with empty, partly demolished, blackhouses. One suspects that a good many of the 200 abandoned blackhouses that we recorded in our survey of the islands are mute testimony to Gordon's clearance, for although the islands' population gradually recovered, it really only did so from the late 1870s onwards, by which time blackhouses as such were no longer being built. By now, houses were being constructed with a fireplace and chimney at one or both ends replacing the old central hearth and hole in the roof.

One of the cleared townships, Balnabodach, has been extensively explored by us. Balnabodach occupies a beautiful site on the southern shore of Loch Obe. Loch Obe is a sea-loch, but its only link to the sea is via a 400m long sea-dyke with steep walls up to 30m high. The dyke is little more than 5m wide at its narrowest point. Loch Obe is therefore both hidden and protected from the sea, and provides a safe

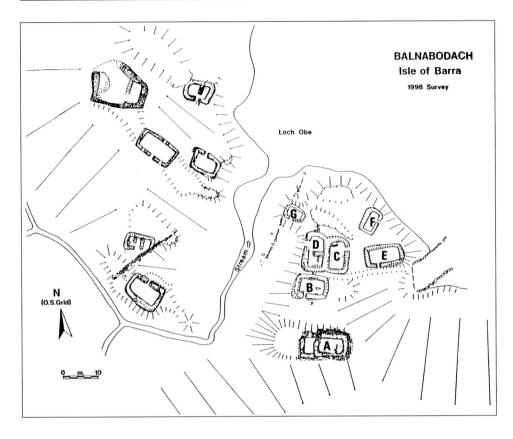

70 Plan of the blackhouse settlement at Balnabodach, Barra; the buildings east of the stream are those cleared in 1851 by Gordon of Cluny

harbourage for small boats. On the south side of the loch there are small areas of pasture and other areas suitable for lazy-bed cultivation plots. The focus of the township in the earlier nineteenth century was by the side of the loch, at the point where a small freshwater stream runs into it (**colour plate 33**).

It was here that we found the remains of 13 buildings, in two groups, one either side of the stream (**70**). The six to the west of the stream have walls which still stand above the turf, sometimes to a height of almost 2m. We know that some of these houses, with fireplaces and chimneys, were built after *c.*1870, and that some were occupied into the 1920s. House F however may have been built earlier than the other houses west of the stream. Its excavation demonstrated that it had a long history as an outbuilding with three structural phases involving sub-divisions, stalls and bins, but it began life as an ordinary blackhouse and initial study of the pottery suggests it may have been a contemporary of the buildings to the east of the stream.

These seven buildings all survived only as low grassed-over humps in the ground and were clearly abandoned long before the buildings to the west. Two of the houses, C and D, were built in a single operation as a semi-detached pair, whilst a third house

71 House A, Balnabodach, as revealed by excavation. It was initially a small single-roomed house, but it was extended at the west end and the extra room apparently used for human occupation

(A) was extended by the addition of a room at its west end to become the largest house in the group (**71**). House G on the other hand was much smaller than any of the other houses, with a single room about 4 x 2.5m in size. Houses A, C and D were all excavated by us, and they yielded pottery, clay pipes, and a few other simple artefacts of the types described in the preceding chapter. The pottery provides the only dating evidence we have for these buildings. It is mostly dated between 1820 and 1860, although there are small quantities of earlier pieces. But does the pottery suggest these homes were cleared in 1850-1?

We can't be sure, because pottery can only be dated in relatively broad brackets, and there is always the problem of valued pieces which are carefully looked after for decades before they get broken and appear in the archaeological deposits. The *median* dates of production for the 51 pots identified never go beyond 1850 but that does not prove that none of the pots was made, let alone broken after that date. However, the absence of even a single sherd of ironstone ware in any of the excavated buildings does suggest they were not occupied after about 1850.

We can place this archaeological evidence alongside that of the census records, parish register and oral traditions. The census of 1841 tells us there were eight house-holds at Balnabodach at that time, and we are tempted to relate these to the seven houses east of the stream, and house F west of the stream. The census describes all of these families as crofters. In the 1851 census not a single one of these families remain, and instead of crofters the township is occupied by fishermen and boat-builders, and a 'farmer' who is not a local Catholic but has come from Ross–shire. This appears to be a classic example of a clearance, with the crofters cleared, the land rented to a farmer, and a group of crofters removed from elsewhere on the island now forced to earn their meagre living from the sea.

Local oral tradition supports this evidence. People were cleared from the rich machair pastures of Eoligarry, Cleit, Greain and Borve, and moved to the east coast. Here they replaced crofters who had already been cleared and sent to Canada. Some were settled at Balnabodach, but others were less fortunate and were put on particularly bleak land at Rulios to the south of Balnabodach. Here there was only rough pasture, peat-lands, and a rugged coastline. Even building stone was in short supply so that these unfortunate crofters had to build houses of turf. Oral tradition says there were up to 20 such 'mud-houses' built down the slope towards the sea, but such structures can soon be reduced to invisibility once they are abandoned to the Hebridean wind and rain. Nevertheless, careful survey of the area in 1999 revealed the traces of four such houses. The best preserved example could be traced around its entire outline and proved to about 10 x 6m overall, with turf walls about 1.3m thick. The only stone seen anywhere in the structure was used to frame the doorway in the north wall.

Oral tradition preserves other memories of traumatic events associated with this enforced migration of the people of Balnabodach. Boats were sent to Northbay to carry off those who had failed to turn up in Lochboisdale on South Uist. One young man of Balnabodach escaped into the hills, but a young girl was less fortunate and was allegedly snatched from milking a cow and carried to the boats with nothing but what she wore. Two other girls, daughters of John Macdougall, miller at Balnabodach, escaped the pursuers, but their father was taken and put aboard the *Admiral*. Elsewhere on Barra, other families were separated in similar circumstances, and with similar results: husbands separated from wives, children from parents, with one forced into hiding on Barra, and the other shipped off to North America.

The enforced emigration of people from Barra and its islands in 1850-1 was not the last time that Barra saw it sons and daughters leave for the New World. From the mid-nineteenth century many voluntarily made their way across the Atlantic to find a new life (**72**), and the migration continued well into the twentieth century. But, equally, the enforced emigration of 1850-1 was by no means the first exodus of Barra people to Canada.

The first Barramen to cross the Atlantic were probably those recruited as soldiers into the Highland regiments who fought in the French Wars. Indeed, General Macneil's grandfather had not only fought in the battle for Quebec but died there of his wounds. Many soldiers returned home when the wars ended, and were able to tell their families and friends about the pros and cons of settling in north America. Others applied for, and were given, land on which to settle themselves. Six Barramen from the 82nd regiment, for example, were settled on land at Malignant Cove, on the north coast of Nova Scotia in 1785.

Across the waters of the Gulf of St Lawrence, on Prince Edward Island, other settlers from Barra were already well established. They had arrived there on the ship

72 Emigrants for Quebec in the mid-nineteenth century, paying their own passage and voluntarily seeking a new life. After Illustrated London News

Alexander in 1772 as part of a group of Catholic emigrants under the leadership of John Macdonald of Glenaladale. He had given each of the settlers a lease on 150 acres of land to be held for 3000 years!

These early Barra pioneers were soon followed by others, in a steady stream in which there were sudden surges. In 1790, 28 Barra families, about 100 people, arrived on the *Queen of Greenock* at Charlottetown, Prince Edward Island. In 1801, the *Sarah* and the *Dove* arrived at Pictou in Nova Scotia with a combined passenger list of about 570 persons, none of whom came from Barra. But other records reveal that about 500 additional emigrants from Barra were picked up, presumably after the ships left Fort William. The following year the *Hector* sailed into Pictou with another 370 people from Barra. In 1817 the *William Tell* and the *Hope* took perhaps as many as 700 people from Barra to Sydney in Cape Breton. More people left Barra on the *Dunlop* in 1818 and the *Harmony* in 1821. Many of these migrants were recruited for emigration by agents, but others simply seized opportunities as they arose. All in all, we believe that more than 2000 Barra people emigrated to Cape Breton, Nova Scotia, and Prince Edward Island over the period from 1770 to 1840.

Since the population of the islands continued to grow through this period, however, it is difficult to identify the material affects of this prolonged episode of emigration in the archaeological landscape. Despite this the Parish register, and both parish and land allotment records from Nova Scotia, do allow us to identify the departure of families from settlements on the islands, and their arrival in Canada.

Using this evidence we have been able to trace the gradual abandonment of the blackhouse settlement at Gortein on the south coast of Ben Tangaval. In the early years of the nineteenth century this was a well populated settlement with perhaps as many as ten families living here. At the core of the settlement was a group of four blackhouses with associated walled lazy-bedded cultivation plots. To the east were three larger blackhouses, and to the west three smaller ones. In the valley behind the settlement were various sheep enclosures and a complex of walls to control the movement of sheep and cattle. There was also a communal drying shed for barley, and a kelp oven down near the beach.

From the parish register we can trace the gradual decline in births in the settlement. Families begin to disappear from the register around 1820. In some cases they subsequently turn up elsewhere on the island, but in others they do not resurface anywhere in Barra. The last recorded birth in Gortein is in 1830 and we believe the settlement was completely abandoned before 1835. Careful searching through the records in public and private archives in Nova Scotia, and cross-checking with the Barra parish register has allowed us to trace the emigration of at least three of the families from Gortien.

Angus and Mary Maclean and their six children, together with John and Margaret Mackinnon and their three children, emigrated around 1820-2. They probably sailed on the ship *Harmony* in 1821, landing at Sydney before moving south to settle around the great Bras D'Or lake where there were already many migrant families from Barra and South Uist. The Macleans obtained land at Boisdale, and the Mackinnons found a new home in the Straits of Barra less than 20 miles to the south. They were followed around 1826 by Archie and Mary Mackinnon with five children, who eventually settled on the other side of the St Andrews Channel to Boisdale, at Point Clear (**73**).

The landscapes which greeted these emigrants when they arrived in Canada were in some respects not unlike those they had left behind in the Western Isles. The rugged, indented coastline and hilly interior of Cape Breton must have looked comfortingly familiar to the emigrants as they approached it from the sea at the end of their two- to three-month passage across the Atlantic. And Cape Breton was, after all, an island on the Atlantic fringe just like their beloved Barra. But there were other Hebridean landscapes which they would never set eyes on in Cape Breton. Gone forever were the lush green grasslands of the machair, covered in early summer with a rich and colourful array of wild flowers. Gone were the huge white shell-sand beaches and offshore tidal islets. And gone too were the open spaces of bleak but beautiful peat moorlands from which one could see for miles in every direction – to the Uists in the north, to Skye, Rum, and Eigg in the east, to Mingulay and Barra Head in the south, and out into the endless Atlantic to the west.

Whereas Barra, the largest of the southern isles, is only eight miles long and seven wide at its extremities, Cape Breton, in contrast, is about 110 x 80 miles. The difference in the scale of the landscape must have been psychologically daunting to the new-comers. Paradoxically, however, this seemingly vast expanse of island must also have been positively claustrophobic for the migrants. The Barra

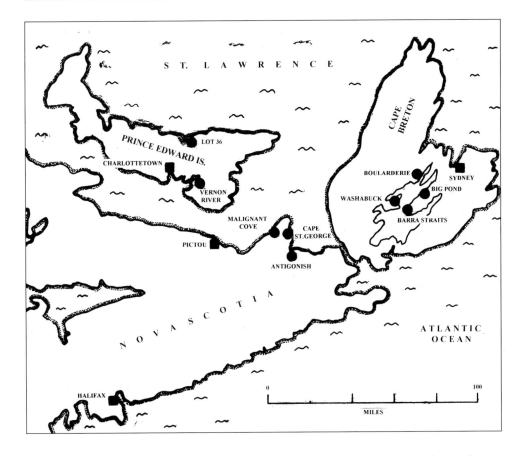

73 *Map of Prince Edward Island, Nova Scotia and Cape Breton, with ports of entry for immigrants (squares) and places particularly associated with immigrants from Barra and the Bishop's Isles (circles)*

islands are notoriously tree-less; Cape Breton (and to the south, Nova Scotia) is covered in trees, even today. The dark pine forests and mixed woodland that cloak the hills and extend right down to the shores still often seem impenetrable, even after two and a half centuries of settlement and exploitation. Coming from the wide open spaces of the southern isles, the new landscape must have seemed forbidding and daunting. Their reactions to it are remembered in some of the Gaelic songs composed by migrants who speak of 'the gloom of the forest . . . with wolves and beasts howling in every cranny', and describe the back-breaking efforts to clear it for growing crops: 'piling tree-trunks on top of each other in bonfires has strained every muscle in my back'.

To add to the miseries they endured in coming to terms with and taming the forest, there was also the Canadian winter to be faced. Although the Western Isles are wet and windy, thanks to the Gulf Stream they have relatively mild winters. In particular snow is something of a rarity. Imagine how unprepared the new

145

Hebridean migrants were for the deep snows, frozen lakes and harbours, heavy frosts and freezing winds which are commonplace around the mouth of the St Lawrence each winter.

In spite of these adversities however the migrants prospered. The land, once cleared of trees, proved extremely fertile and productive for growing grain, potatoes and vegetables. Around the shores of the lakes were pastures for sheep and cattle, and duck and geese to hunt. In the forests were moose, caribou and deer. And the rivers and seas were exceptionally rich in seafood, cod, herring, mackerel, salmon, oysters and lobsters. There was no longer the need to spend long hours collecting kelp. Nor were the summer days taken up with cutting, drying and transporting peat – the forests provided all the fuel needed for the household fire throughout the winter.

The building of the house itself, however, again required the settlers to learn new skills and adapt to a totally new building material. Not only was loose stone relatively scarce, but reason demanded that the trees being felled to clear the land should be put to good use to build a house and outbuildings. But for the majority of the people from the southern isles, building in wood was a totally new experience. Wood was so scarce on Barra and its islands that the people not only had no experience of using it as a building material, but they had no woodworking tools of any sort. To begin with they must have relied on the advice and goodwill of the existing settlers, who taught them to build the basic log-cabin (**colour plate 34**). In size and internal simplicity the cabins were very similar to the Barra blackhouses, with the one difference that they had a fireplace and chimney at one end rather than a hearth in the middle of the room and a hole in the roof above it.

Having secured their food and shelter, the migrants then set about familiarising their new landscapes and embedding their culture in its new setting. Different as the landscape around Grand Narrows may have been from that of Barra, we nevertheless find a plethora of place-names recalling the places and faces of the homeland – Barra Glen, Castle Bay, Macneils Vale, Mackinnons Harbour, Macdougalls Point. Macneils, Mackinnons and Macdougalls had been amongst the 20 or so Barra families who had sailed into Pictou on the Hector in 1802 and settled around Grand Narrows in 1804-5. These same settlers then worked together to build their first church, a modest timber structure only 11 x 6m, down by the shore of Barra Straits in 1815.

The maintenance of their religion was important to these Catholic people; it was both a source of comfort and support when times were bad, and part of the social cement which held their communities together. Closely intertwined with the practise of their religion was the maintenance of their native, Gaelic, language. Although in Cape Breton they mixed far more with English (and indeed French) speakers than they ever had in the Western Isles, they clung to their Gaelic tenaciously. It was used in church, and it was used for songs at family gatherings and for storytelling around the hearth in the winter, just as it always had been back in the southern isles. And of course it was used for recounting family genealogies and stories both of life in the western isles and in the pioneer days in Canada.

74 Blackhouse, byre and drying shed at Brevig, Barra. A large house like this, with both a byre and drying shed alongside may have belonged to a tacksman

These oral family histories, supplemented and checked wherever possible by documentary sources in the Western Isles and in Canada, allow us to trace the story of some of these migrant families from their homes in Barra at the end of the eighteenth century up to the modern day. One such family was the Macneils of Brevig. Roderick Macneil was tacksman of Brevig, as was his father before him. Like most tacksmen, he was a close relative of the chief, from whom he had a grant of land. The portion of it he did not himself farm was rented out to tenants, whose rents he collected. Tacksmen were therefore relatively prosperous members of the island community, and Roderick Macneil of Brevig was presumably no exception.

There is neither oral tradition nor documents that allow us to identify exactly where in Brevig Roderick lived. Around Brevig bay there are the remains of ten blackhouses, four of which are notably larger than the rest and have one or two outbuildings. Roderick's house may be among these. The complex recorded as site S34 gives a good idea of the sort of home we might expect a tacksman to occupy (**74**). The buildings are located on a flat shelf, just above a small but freely flowing stream, in a sheltered depression. Across the stream, upslope from the house, is a rare example of a cultivation plot enclosed by a stone wall. Beyond this is rough pasture. Below the house is a more gently undulating area suitable for pasture and in some places for cultivation, as betrayed by relict lazybeds and clearance cairns. The sea in Brevig Bay is 400m to the south.

The house is 12.5 x 6m overall, well above average on Barra, with a single central doorway and no visible trace of internal partitions. Behind the house is a second building 9 x 6.5m with a raised platform at one end across which a diagonal depression marks the line of a flue. This is a shed for drying the grain. Built against one side of the drying shed is a third building, 8.5 x 4m, with a door in a short end wall through which a depression runs out downslope, marking the line of a drain. This is a byre. Whilst many Barra blackhouses have adjacent byres, few have drying sheds as well, and this whole complex has an air of relative affluence about it.

From a farm like this, in 1801, Roderick's eldest son, Roderick Og, set off with his cousin James Macneil for Greenock, where they negotiated with an emigration agent called Hugh Dunoon, a passage to Pictou for themselves and a large party of Barra people. Subsequently, they sailed on the *Dove* and the *Sarah* respectively, and landed at Pictou in late summer. Whilst many of the Barra emigrants moved on to Cape Breton or to the north shore of Nova Scotia, Roderick Og sought land in Prince Edward Island. Not only had Prince Edward Island been more intensively cleared and farmed than Cape Breton by 1801, but the soil there was particularly fertile.

In 1802 his father and his siblings – two sisters and a younger brother – joined him, sailing on the *Hector*, and they settled into a new life at Vernon River (**colour plate 35**). They acquired a 340 acre plot of land, which ran up the gentle slope from the banks of the Vernon River itself. Roderick, former tacksman of Brevig, eventually died at Vernon River in 1825, in his mid-80s. Roderick Og, who had been school-teaching for a time, was himself now 48 years old with ten children, and had clearly become a respected member of the local community. In 1830 he was elected a representative to the Legislative Assembly of P.E.I. In the census of 1841 his farm is recorded as housing 2 horses, 14 cattle, 12 sheep, and 10 pigs, and producing 14 bushels of wheat, 4 of barley, 325 of oats, and 450 of potatoes. In both the variety of animals and crops, and the quantities produced, this was obviously a far more prosperous farm than the one his father had left behind in Brevig.

Although we have no surviving record of his house at this time, we can be confident it was a far cry from the Brevig blackhouses and the pioneer log-cabins. By around 1830 many migrant families were sufficiently well-off to build impressive two-storey timber houses. The Macdonald house, built in 1829 and preserved in the Highland Village at Iona, Cape Breton, is a good example of the type (**colour plate 36**). It had a central chimney which served back-to-back fireplaces in two main downstairs rooms. There was a separate kitchen downstairs too, and upstairs two or three rooms were used as bedrooms and work room for the spinning wheel and loom. With as many as six windows downstairs and four upstairs, the contrast with the dark interiors of the blackhouses could not be more pronounced.

A recently discovered ledger belonging to a merchant called Macdonald, who had a business at St Peters on the north shore of Prince Edward Island, reveals the sort of goods which successful Scottish emigrants were now able to buy. Between 1813 and 1815, Duncan Gillis purchased muslin, silk and printed cotton, as well as powder and shot, and a supply of iron. Roderick Macdonald's purchases included tobacco, tea, sugar, mugs, cotton, muslin, buttons, handkerchiefs, knives and forks, a lot of writing paper and even more rum! It is difficult to imagine any crofter in Barra in 1815 being able to purchase such a wide array of materials.

The Macneils of Brevig continued to grow and prosper on their land at Vernon River, and they still own the plot to this day, although for part of the year they live in New England. It is 200 years and seven generations since their ancestor Roderick first set eyes on the gentle red-soiled landscape of Prince Edward Island and the broad shallow waters of Vernon River. Yet like hundreds of other north American families whose roots lie in Barra and the Bishop's Isles, they keep alive the tales and the memories of those bleak but beautiful islands on the other side of the Atlantic.

Some sites to visit on Barra and Vatersay

This short guide provides brief instructions on how to find these sites and the main points of interest in each case; more about the history of the sites, and the finds made in excavations on them, can be found by referring to the text of the preceding chapters. Numbers in bold in brackets refer to illustrations of the monument to be found in this book. A six figure National Grid Reference (NGR) is provided and an Ordnance Survey map (Sheet 31) should be used in conjunction with the instructions given here. The order of sites follows a clockwise direction from Castlebay. Remember to respect the crofters' privacy and their fences, using only stiles or gates to cross boundaries.

Castlebay

The main site in Castlebay is, of course, Kisimul Castle (**52**), which stands on a rocky islet near the ferry terminal. Since Historic Scotland took over custody of the castle, it can be visited most days in the summer season, the visit including a short boat trip and guided tour. Although heavily restored, it provides a good idea of what the castle was like in the fifteenth and sixteenth centuries.

While in Castlebay, if you take the road westwards from the 'Square', within 200m you pass, on the right, the former schoolhouse where the Crofting Commission met in 1883. Another 300m on is the new Heritage Centre, where in addition to changing displays on aspects of the island's history, finds from the Neolithic site at Alt Chrisal are displayed.

Tangaval and Vatersay

About a kilometre along the ring road west of Castlebay, at Nask, there is a left turn onto the road to Vatersay. After climbing a steepish hill, there is pull-in area from where Vatersay (and beyond it Sandray) can be viewed. Shortly after this on the downhill descent, an unusual small passage grave (**15**) is preserved above the road fence (NL647977).

About 100m after the cattle grid at the bottom of the hill is the site of Alt Chrisal (NL643977). Enter through the metal gate and turn right to cross the stream. The excavated blackhouse (**64**) is clear to see, and next to it the more crudely built byre (**65**). Just behind the blackhouse some of the excavated features of the neolithic settlement can be seen (**6, 7**) including two hearths and the 'patio'. From here, cross the stream and gradually climb up the slope following the line of the stream. You will come to a small sub-circular hut, and just above it a larger one. This is the hut (**9**) in which a complete Beaker (**10**) was found in the cist attached to its back wall. From the hut walk back towards the road but diagonally right (away from the stream line). You will come downslope to the big Iron Age wheelhouse with its seven radiating piers (**33, 34**).

Returning to the road follow it and cross the Vatersay causeway. After 800m the low conical hill on which Dun Caolis (NL629971) sits will be on your right. This is well worth a visit, though unexcavated (**41**). Careful examination reveals the covering slabs of the gallery of this broch tower and note the massive blocks of stone used in the wall. Note also the later rectangular houses (medieval?) built around the broch.

Opposite Dun Caolis, a trackway leaves the road past a small cottage. About 400m along this track, where there are two very small rocky islets in the sea, a passage grave (**16**) is set about 80m upslope (NL635969). Note the V-shaped entrance to the passage and the remains of the stone cairn which once covered it.

Continuing along the road towards Vatersay village, the road swings south to run along the edge of Vatersay Bay. At NL642947 the aerial archaeology of the island is represented by the remains of a Catalina flying-boat which crashed into the hill above the road in 1944. Leaving the road by the community hall, it is worth crossing the machair to West Bay (Bagh Siar) if only for the view and the beach. But on the dunes above the beach is the monument to the 350 souls who perished when a nineteenth-century emigrant ship the *Annie Jane* was driven onto the headland. They were buried in the dunes beneath the monument. From here one can walk south along the beach, and ascend the slope towards the site of Dun Vatersay.

This stands on a prominent (and windy) hilltop (NL627945), with wonderful views in all directions. Immediately below to the west you can see the outline of the excavated Bronze Age kerbed cairn (**20-4**); if you visit it, see if you can find the kerbs of the other unexcavated three cairns in this cemetery.

The West Coast

Proceeding along the ring road west from Nask, Loch St Clair is passed on the left with the medieval tower (NL647996) standing on an islet near the shore. After another kilometre the Borve valley opens out to the right, and Borve headland to the left. Entrance to the headland is through a gate, and if the track is followed (past the stump of a surviving standing stone, NF653014) it leads to the cemetery. In the south-east corner is a prominent mound with its original wall still visible beneath the cemetery wall. This is an Iron Age broch, and it may be associated with a curious triangular embanked enclosure with upright stones set in its bank, at the edge of the headland (NF646017).

Returning to the road, a right turn at the next junction (by Craigston school) leads up into the valley. If the road, and then the track, is followed to the end it leads to the 'blackhouse museum', which is in fact a small whitehouse, with chimney. It provides a fascinating insight into the homes of the Barra crofters around 1900. From here one can follow the croft fence lines uphill to the great Neolithic tomb of Dun Bharpa (NF672019). This still stands 5m high and although unexcavated its entrance passage and chamber can just be made out; its most impressive feature is the ring of upright monoliths erected around its circumference. A fallen standing stone lies about 50m to the north-west just beyond the head-dyke.

The enthusiast can trek 700m south-westwards and gradually downslope from Dun Bharpa to reach a second neolithic passage grave at Balnacraig (NF676012). The cairn and part of the chamber have been robbed to build first an Iron Age round-house (just about visible to the north of the tomb), then a sequence of probably medieval and early modern shieling huts, and finally an early modern boundary wall.

Eoligarry peninsula

From the famous tidal airfield, a walk through the dunes and southwards along the wonderful beach of Traigh Eais leads over a low grassy headland and to a path which skirts the foot of Ben Erival. Following this for 500m, you come to the site of Dun Clieff (NF682053), a late Iron Age roundhouse on a very exposed tidal islet.

The road north from the airfield branches in two soon after Eoligarry school-house, and the left-hand fork leads to the early Christian church and chapels at Kilbarr (NF705074). Apart from the remains of the church, the late medieval grave slabs and replica of the Norse memorial stone housed in the renovated north chapel are worth seeing (**54, 55**). Compton Mackenzie is buried in the churchyard.

Following the road towards the north tip of the island, the site of Dun Scurrival (**37**) overlooks the road where it turns a sharp right (NF695081). A steep climb through the pastures leads to a mass of tumbled masonry from the walls of this Iron Age 'dun'. Its exact form and nature is uncertain, but it had a double wall, like a broch, visible on its northern side and there are traces of structures inside it too.

East coast

At Northbay, a track up the side of the church leads to the present-day presbytery. The wall which surrounds its garden is the original wall of General Macneil's 'chemical factory', built around 1830. If you go down the side of it to the edge of the water you will see the blocked portals through which kelp and peat were delivered by water to the factory.

A turning left to Bruernish soon after leaving Northbay leads to the site of another 'dun', in this case quite certainly a double-walled broch tower (NF715027), standing on a tidal islet. It was approached by a rough causeway, which can be crossed (by the intrepid) at low tide.

The ring road from Northbay then swings around the end of Loch Obe, and climbs a gentle hill. The site of the 'clearance' settlement of Balnabodach is down by the shore of the Loch at NF715017. To the east of the small stream are the low remains of the 'cleared' settlement (**70, 71**) including houses excavated by the Sheffield team, which overlie traces of both Neolithic and Iron Age settlement on the same spot. To the west are the houses built after the clearances, including the 'plague house', its windows still blocked-up, built *c*.1881 and abandoned after two deaths from typhoid in 1894.

Finally, at Brevig, the only still-erect standing stone of any size on the island can be found at NL689990, with the smashed remains of a second stone alongside.

Bibliography

The detailed reports on our work in the Western Isles are published in three monographs:

K. Branigan and P. Foster *Barra: Archaeological Research on Ben Tangaval* (Sheffield Academic Press) 1995

K. Branigan and P. Foster *From Barra to Berneray* (Sheffield Academic Press) 2000

D. Gilberston, M. Kent and J. Grattan *The Outer Hebrides: the Last 14,000 Years* (Sheffield Academic Press) 1996

A fourth volume in the SEARCH series provides important new information on the Iron Age in the Western Isles:

M. Parker Pearson and N. Sharples *Between Land and Sea* (Sheffield Academic Press) 1999

A fifth volume focussing on the historical period and the emigrations to north America is due for publication in 2003.

Other books concerned with the archaeology and history of Barra and the Bishop's Isles are very few but include:

B. Buxton *Mingulay: An Island and its People* (Birlinn) 1995

J.L. Campbell (ed.) *The Book of Barra* (reprint, Acair) 1998

Three journal articles may also be mentioned:

K. Branigan and C. Merrony 'The Hebridean blackhouse on the Isle of Barra' *Scottish Archaeol. J.* 22 (2000) 1-16

A. Young 'An aisled farmhouse at the Allasdale' *Proc. Soc. of Antiquaries Scotland* 87 (1952) 80-106

A. Young 'Excavations at Dun Cuier' *Proc. of Soc. of Antiquaries Scotland* 89 (1955) 290-328

Books concerned with the archaeology of the Outer Hebrides which provide further information on Barra and its islands as well as putting them into a wider context include:

I. Armit *The Late Prehistory of the Western Isles* (British Archaeol. Reports) BS 221, 1992

I. Armit *The Archaeology of Skye and the Western Isles* (Edinburgh Univ. Press) 1996

Books providing an overview of the Norse, medieval and early modern periods include:

B.E. Crawford *Scandinavian Scotland* (Leicester University Press) 1997

R. Dodgshon *From Chiefs to Landlords* (Edinburgh University Press) 1998

R.A. Macdonald *The Kingdom of the Isles: Scotland's Western Seaboard c.1100 - c.1336* (Tuckwell Press) 1997

Books about the period of the clearances and emigration include:

J. Bumstead *The People's Clearances* (Edinburgh University Press) 1982

J.L. Campbell *Songs Remembered in Exile* (revised second edition Birlinn) 1999

T. Devine *The Great Highland Famine* (John Donald) 1988

Glossary

aisled house A circular house with free-standing radial piers; usually Middle Iron Age in date and sunk down into the ground, on Barra most examples are built above ground level. See also **wheelhouse**.

blackhouse A thick-walled, low, oblong house with rounded corners. The wall is stone-faced but packed with an earth and turf core. The hearth is in the middle of the floor and there are no chimneys, only a hole in the roof. Extant examples are mainly eighteenth- and nineteenth-century in date, and the origins of the type are still obscure.

broch A tower-like stone-built structure with an inner and outer wall separated by a narrow gallery on each floor. Mostly Middle Iron Age in date, and found mostly in western and northern Scotland.

cist a stone-lined pit or 'box', usually with walls of slabs set on edge. Mostly used for burials but also found in domestic contexts.

Clearances The enforced removal of crofters from their crofts sometimes to other areas, but often by complete eviction. In Barra and its islands, the main Clearance was in 1850-1, under the orders of Colonel Gordon of Cluny, the then owner of the estate.

clearance cairns Small mounds of stones which have been removed from cultivation plots to improve their productivity and ease of cultivation.

dun Borrowed from the Gaelic for a 'fort', dun has become a term of convenience for substantial stone-built structures and enclosures, usually oval or sub-circular, which cannot be readily identified as brochs, wheelhouses or roundhouses.

kerbed cairn A stone cairn with a well-defined kerb around its perimeter, in which the tops of the kerb stones are all set at more or less the same level. Excavated examples prove to cover cremation burials of the Bronze Age. If the cairn has a setting of perimeter stones which form an undulating 'kerb' the authors call them 'bordered cairns'.

machair Lime-rich soils with a shell-rich blown sand base, supporting grasslands characterised by mostly native flora, found along the coastal margins of the islands.

passage grave A stone-built tomb in which a passage leads to a burial chamber (though the distinction between passage and chamber is often blurred, particularly in small examples). The chambers, and usually the passages, are built with large stone slabs and both are covered by a stone cairn. Built and used in the later fourth and third millennia BC.

shieling   A seasonal campsite, with temporary huts built of stone and turf, used by those looking after cattle and sheep on the higher or more remote summer pastures.

wheelhouse   Similar construction to an **aisled house** but with the piers joined to the circular wall of the house, so that there is no perimeter 'aisle'. In fact many wheelhouses prove to have been built as aisled houses, and the piers to have been extended to meet the perimeter wall during the building's occupation.

Index